RISEN INDEED!

Meditations on the Resurrection of Christ

TOM KINGERY

WESTBOW
PRESS®
A DIVISION OF THOMAS NELSON
& ZONDERVAN

WestBow Press books may be ordered through booksellers or by contacting:

WestBow Press
A Division of Thomas Nelson & Zondervan
1663 Liberty Drive
Bloomington, IN 47403
www.westbowpress.com
844-714-3454

ISBN: 978-1-6642-7408-2 (sc)
ISBN: 978-1-6642-7409-9 (e)

Library of Congress Control Number: 2022914041

Print information available on the last page.

WestBow Press rev. date: 8/3/2022

INTRODUCTION

I am the resurrection and the life.
Those who believe in me, even though they die, will live,
and everyone who lives and believes in me will never die.

—JOHN 11:25–26

The resurrection is three things: It is proof. It is power. And it is promise.

PROOF

The resurrection proves that Jesus is Lord. He is who He said He was in John 11: "I am the resurrection and the life" (v. 25). It proves that Jesus is the Christ, the Messiah, the Savior of the world. It proves God's love for us, as in "God so loved the world that he gave his only Son, so that everyone who believes in him may not perish but have eternal life" (John 3:16). The resurrection of Jesus proves to us that we need not doubt, that we can trust what we believe, and that we can have confidence in our faith.

In Acts chapter 17, Paul was in Athens. He testified about the one true God and said that everyone needed to repent because "he has fixed a day on which he will have the world judged in righteousness by a man whom he appointed, and of this he has given assurance to all by raising him from the dead" (17:31). That assurance is the validation of the resurrection in a believer's heart. And it is our assurance in the judgment!

Earlier in Acts, Paul testified that after Jesus fulfilled what the prophets had written of the Messiah by dying on the cross and then being laid in a tomb: "God raised him up from the dead; and for many days he appeared to those who came up with Him from Galilee to Jerusalem, and they are now his witnesses to the people" (Acts 13:30–31). The fact that there were witnesses of the risen and living body of Jesus reveals the proof we need. And we can be witnesses too.

Some will say that they were perpetuating a lie. *They* might say, "Jesus had not really risen." "He had not come to life again." But the witnesses were willing to die for this truth. People would not die for a lie! You would think that someone would have come clean somewhere along the line just to clear their conscience and admit that they were speaking falsehoods, perpetuating a hoax. But the changed lives of all those disciples, and those who believed because of *their* witness, and even of *my* faith today is a testimony to the reality of the resurrection. And you can testify too.

Paul wrote to the Corinthians: "I handed on to you as of first importance what I in turn had received: that Christ died for our sins in accordance with the scriptures, and that he was buried, and that he was raised on the third day in accordance with the scriptures, and that he appeared to Cephas, then to the twelve. Then he appeared to more than five hundred brothers and sisters at one time" (1 Corinthians 15:3–6). "Last of all, as to one untimely born, he appeared also to me" (v. 8). And He is here for us today!

What do we do with this truth? Do we think of this testimony as just a part of a "story"? Is it fiction? Is it just a part of a plot to make themselves look good? Many of those early believers died for what they claimed to be true. And what nonbelievers want to do is deny *their* testimony. But there was a way they could have proved it was a lie: produce the dead body of Jesus!

Without the dead body of Jesus, the resurrection cannot be proven false! The resurrection is the proof that Jesus is the Christ! Whatever doubts we may have because it is supposedly "too good to be true," or just too amazing, can be overcome by trusting in the testimony of the first witnesses, then, the witness of those who believed *their* testimony, and of those who believed in *theirs*, and … of *mine*! I believe it. I trust the testimony of the almost two thousand years of believers who have trusted it. And you can trust it too!

The resurrection proves that Jesus is Lord!

POWER

The resurrection is a power in my life, and, in the heart of every believer! There is power in someone's testimony as they give witness to the glory of God in their experience of Christ. Paul said, "I want to know Christ and the power of his resurrection and the sharing of his sufferings by becoming like him in his death, if somehow I may attain the resurrection from the dead" (Philippians 3:10–11).

What *is* the "power of his resurrection?" Look here: "In the world ye shall have tribulation, but be of good cheer; I have overcome the world" (John 16:33 KJV). Consider the power of a faith in Christ that can say with Paul:

> If God is for us, who is against us? He who did not withhold his own Son, but gave him up for all of us, will he not with him also give us everything else? Who will bring any charge against God's elect? It is God who justifies. Who is to condemn? It is Christ Jesus, who died, yes, who was raised, who is at the right hand of God, who indeed intercedes for us. Who will separate us from the love of Christ? Will hardship, or distress, or persecution, or famine, or nakedness, or peril, or sword?

As it is written, "For your sake we are being killed all day long; we are accounted as sheep to be slaughtered" (Psalm 44:22).

> No, in all these things we are more than conquerors through him who loved us. For I am convinced that neither death, nor life, nor angels, nor rulers, nor things present, nor things to come, nor powers, nor height, nor depth, nor anything else in all creation will be able to separate us from the love of God in Christ Jesus our Lord. (Romans 8:37–39)

That's a power we claim by faith. We are conquerors! Because of the resurrection, we are never going to be defeated! Nothing can work against us! We can overcome the world!

Peter, on the day of Pentecost, proclaimed of Christ: "But God raised him up, having freed him from death, because it was impossible for him to be held in its power" (Acts 2:24).

And this power is upon us!

But if we have died with Christ, we believe that we will live with him. We know that Christ, being raised from the dead, will never die again; death no longer has dominion over him. The death he died, he died to sin, once for all but the life he lives, he lives to God. So you also must consider yourselves dead to sin and alive to God in Christ Jesus. (Romans 6:8–11)

The resurrection power is a power over sin, and by faith, that power is upon us! Rejoice!

PROMISE

The resurrection is a promise from God to every believer!

Start with the promise of Jesus in John 11. Jesus has told Mary and Martha, "Your brother will rise again" (v. 23). Martha then expressed the contemporary view at the time: "I know that he will rise again in the resurrection on the last day" (v. 24). The belief was that at the end of time an "awakening" would occur, and the dead would come to life! Catch the vision of Daniel:

At that time Michael, the great prince, the protector of your people, shall arise. There shall be a time of anguish, such as has never occurred since nations first came into existence. But, at that time your people shall be delivered, everyone who is found written in the book. Many of those who sleep in the dust of the earth shall awake, some to everlasting life, and some to shame and everlasting contempt. Those who are wise shall shine like the brightness of the sky, and those who lead many to righteousness, like the stars forever and ever. (Daniel 12:1–3)

It is after Martha expresses her belief that Jesus opens her mind a bit more: "I am the resurrection and the life. Those who believe in me, even though they die, will live, and everyone who lives and believes in me will never die" (John 11:25–26).

What a beautiful promise!

Here's another promise:

> Do you not know that all of us who have been baptized
> into Christ Jesus were baptized into his death? Therefore
> we have been buried with him by baptism into death, so
> that, just as Christ was raised from the dead by the glory
> of the Father, so we too might walk in newness of life.
> For if we have been united with him in a death like his,
> we will certainly be united with him in a resurrection like
> his. (Romans 6:3–5)

"But if we have died with Christ, we believe that we will also live with
him." (v. 8) The promise of Paul's testimony is an inspiration! Trust it.

Paul repeats this promise in First Thessalonians: "Since we believe that
Jesus died and rose again, even so, through Jesus, God will bring with him
those who have died" (4:14).

In Ephesians, we see the testimony of the promise expressed
wonderfully:

> I pray that the God of our Lord Jesus Christ, the Father
> of glory, may give you a spirit of wisdom and revelation
> as you come to know him, so that, with the eyes of
> your heart enlightened, you may know what is the hope
> to which he has called you, what are the riches of his
> glorious inheritance among the saints, and what is the
> immeasurable greatness of his power for us who believe,
> according to the working of his great power. God put
> this power to work in Christ when he raised him from
> the dead and seated him at his right hand in the heavenly
> places, far above all rule and authority and power and
> dominion, and above every name that is named, not only
> in this age but also in the age to come. And he has put all
> things under his feet and has made him the head over all

things for the church, which is his body, the fullness of him who fills all in all. (1:17–23)

And Paul goes on to say: "God, who is rich in mercy, out of the great love with which he loved us even when we were dead through our trespasses, made us alive together with Christ—by grace you have been saved—and raised us up with him" (Ephesians 2:4–6).

"Blessed be the God and Father of our Lord Jesus Christ! By his great mercy he has given us a new birth into a living hope through the resurrection of Jesus Christ from the dead, and into an inheritance that is imperishable, undefiled, and unfading, kept in heaven for you" (1 Peter 1:3–5).

AN INVITATION

The promises, the power, and the proof of the resurrection ignite a fire for those who believe. Hope is inspired, and faith is encouraged. I am encouraged. And I want to share my meditations on the resurrection of Christ in this book. As if in a gallery of paintings or images that the resurrection has moved me to create, let them appear through me; come and see what is offered. Don't enter this gallery to analyze every offering, although that's okay. My hope is that at least some of the meditations will capture your heart and mind and encourage your belief. If anything, at least you will view another piece of my heart. I hope that *that*, in itself, will be worth the viewing.

May God bless us all in our journeys as we experience the risen Christ. "Risen indeed!"

PART 1
Enter the Gallery

We can feel resurrection.

The first image to be encountered in this special gallery is that of a father with one of his grown sons. The father is around fifty years old, the son about thirty. The son is bigger, more solid, hearty, and a bit ruffled. He's been working all day and is a bit dirty and worn. He is responsible and coordinates well the team of servants on the father's great estate.

The son is looking away from the father, away from the front of their home. His hands are clenched on his hips, and he has a look of disdain in his eyes. The father has one hand on the son's shoulder, and with the other he is reaching toward the house. More light than usual is coming from within. Musicians are there, and the joyful sound of a party is going on.

The father is appealing to his older son, who seems to defy the idea of going inside. The father is saying, "This brother of yours was dead and has come to life ... He was lost and has been found" (Luke 15:32).

I believe we can understand the resurrection of Christ because we know what it is like to experience someone who was "dead" return to life. For the brother of the prodigal son, his father's younger son was still dead to him. The hope is that the older son will come to believe in the "new life" of his younger brother.

MEDITATION 1

My Son Was Dead
and Is Alive Again

But the father said to his slaves,
"Quickly, bring out a robe
—the best one—
and put it on him;
put a ring on his finger and sandals on his feet.
And get the fatted calf and boil it,
and let us eat and celebrate;
for this son of mine was dead and is alive again;
he was lost and is found!"
And they began to celebrate.

(LUKE 15:22–24)

In many respects, we can project the father's memories of his prodigal son into our midst. I think most parents, when they think of their children, recall every moment of their lives, not just today. Their children will always be those bundles of joy that they held in their arms as well as the accomplished leaders they have become; they are the toddlers learning to walk and the adults running the show; they are the teenagers coming of age as well as the mature and responsible people they have become. The prodigal son's father did not dwell on the current mess his son had made of his life. Rather, he longed for the gift he had been. The father's eyes often scanned the horizon down the lane, wishing he could see the boy coming back. This picture is a part of that wonderful moment when his son returned home.

"This son of mine was dead and is alive again!" (Luke 15:24).

The eighty-year-old woman who lived in the house just west of ours as I was growing up was Ovida Nelson. My mother called her "Wid." She could talk about her husband, Victor, as if he was still in the room with her. But he'd been dead for several years. One time, she told my mother that remembering Victor made her feel like he was alive again.

She could feel resurrection.

With the story of the prodigal son (Luke 15:11–32), Jesus gives us a new way of looking at life with its failures and triumphs. When we can see beyond the shortcomings in someone's life and overcome that dead-to-me attitude, someone's existence takes on a whole new meaning. Likewise, we can gain a new way of looking at death. When someone is no longer with us, our memories can bring them back to life (to some degree). I'm not just talking about nostalgia but the feeling. Someone can be present to us in some very real ways.

We can feel resurrection.

Consider life. Are there any barriers between you and God? Realize the hope of Romans 8:38–39: "For I am convinced that neither death, nor life, nor angels, nor rulers, nor things present, nor things to come, nor powers, not height, nor depth, nor anything else in all creation, will be able to separate us from the love of God in Christ Jesus our Lord."

Death might seem to separate us. It is a threat to life and to the living. Though the prodigal son felt *secure*, he learned how fragile the future can be. Though he felt like he was in control, he saw his life spin into chaos. And when he confronted life's vulnerabilities, he experienced failure. And yet, through that failure, he began to see the chance to start over. He began to feel resurrection.

And he learned that if you try to play it cool, you can turn into ice.

Consider death. Death is not the enemy we think it is. The real enemy is fear. We will all learn that there is no control over the unknown. And we often fear the unknown. What are the unknowns in death? To die is to lose life. So, death is sad. To die is to *leave* life behind. So, death is lonely. To die is to end life in this world. So, death can be very frustrating, especially when life, for whatever reason, seems unfinished.

We need something that can finish our lives! We need resurrection.

Consider the resurrection of Christ. "My son is alive again!" Repentance, at least the repentance of the prodigal son, is like rising from the dead! We can find new life! Didn't someone once say that to get to the kingdom of sunshine and rainbows, we need to learn to see in the dark? The resurrection of Christ gives us a new way of seeing! The way may start low, but to get higher, we need to go deep. We need a new way of looking at death. It is not an end but a beginning. It is not final. We are just starting.

Wonder, for a moment, what the world would be like if Jesus had never risen from the dead. When we die or when someone else dies, would we ask ourselves, "Is that all there is?" We need proof of something more. Would we feel hopeless? We need the promise of something beyond this world. Would we feel all too vulnerable? We need something that empowers us in our weakness. Here it is:

If we have been united with him in a death like his, we will certainly be united with him in a resurrection like his. We know that our old self was crucified with him so that the body of sin might be destroyed, and we might no longer be enslaved to sin. For whoever has died is freed from sin. But if we have died with Christ, we believe that we will also live with him. We know that Christ, being raised from the dead, will never die again; death no longer has dominion over him. The death he died, he died to sin, once for all; but the life he lives, he lives to God. So, you also must consider yourselves dead to sin and alive to God in Christ Jesus (Romans 6:5–11).

Because He Lives

There is no fear in love,
but perfect love casts out fear.

—1 JOHN 4:18

Because He lives, we who believe live too! Death is not an evil to be wary of, nor is it an unknown to be feared. Death is a change from life to Life. We trust this because Jesus lives. "An empty grave is there to prove my savior lives!" (hymn "Because He Lives"). We believe this because the power of the resurrection is upon us. It is a power we experience whenever we are renewed, whenever we see the transforming grace of love and hope and forgiveness. And we who believe are part of the renewing grace at work in the world. "For the law of the Spirit of Life in Christ Jesus has set us free from the law of sin and of death!" (Romans 8:2).

"Because He lives, I can face tomorrow" (hymn "Because He Lives"). However uncertain tomorrow may seem, Christ is with us. We are not alone. No matter how unpredictable the future may be, we can trust the guidance of the Holy Comforter; we can depend on the love of God in Jesus Christ, and we can rely on the grace and goodness we have witnessed in our Lord.

We live in a world where there are great anxieties in life for many. Some look ahead to tomorrow, wondering where they will get the food that they need just to live another day. Some may live with great instabilities in their lives. They wonder whether an unsolicited attack may come their way from those who, for whatever reasons, harbor hatred toward them. Some may be facing great trials or painful procedures that make them queasy at the prospect of taking physical risks, or, at minimum, they are uneasy about their vulnerabilities. But …

"Because He lives all fear is gone" (hymn "Because He Lives"). We are not hopeless. The things that frighten us are nothing compared to the immense power and love of God. Whatever misgivings we may have had, we who love God have learned that "there is no fear in love … perfect love casts out fear!" (1 John 4:18). And God's love in Christ is perfect! In fact, our faith can make us bold! (1 John 4:17).

When all fear is gone, a risk no longer seems like a gamble but like an adventure. And so, our ventures onto new paths can be a great source of excitement. And for those who face tomorrow with grave uncertainties, we are there for them. The church is a source of both hope and optimism. And there is a reason for our confidence.

"Because I know He holds the future" (hymn "Because He Lives"). The power of the resurrection is experienced in the way we have witnessed God pulling Christ through—through the agony of His Passion, through the humility of His Crucifixion, and through the desolation of His death. God pulled Jesus through it all! And God will pull us through. We are restored by Christ's reconciling act of obedience and suffering. We are revived by Christ's redeeming grace. And we are renewed by Christ's resurrection power.

Accept this in your life, and I guarantee it will make a wonderful difference. Our whole way of looking at life, our whole outlook, with all of life's anxieties, trials, and uncertainties, will be based on our reason for confidence, not on fears left by a limited human understanding of the way things are. And the way things are has changed because of the resurrection.

"And life is worth the living just because He lives" (hymn "Because He Lives"). In spite of our vulnerabilities, regardless of how fragile we may feel, and notwithstanding our frailties, we have learned that God's power is made perfect in our weakness! (2 Corinthians 12:9) It is better to truly live our lives in the light of our knowledge of Christ, than to half-heartedly eke out a protected existence of minimum vitality! It is better to live life to the fullest with the power of the resurrection upon us, than to just claim heaven by and by as if we did not taste it already!

If He lives, then He reigns! And if He reigns, then He is in control! He *is* in control! Let Him have you! We have Him!

"I know that my redeemer lives!" (Job 19:25 NIV).

"Because He Lives." Words by Gloria, Music by William Gaither. Copyright c 1971 William J. Gailhet Inc. ASCAP. (Hymn: U4738 Warner Press Inc. USA)

Christ the Lord Is Risen Today!

Since you have been raised with Christ,
set your hearts on the things that are above,
where Christ is seated at the right hand of God.
Set your minds on things that are above, not on earthly things.

–COLOSSIANS 3:1–2

Let's not approach Easter as if we didn't already know about the resurrection; not as if we *were* learning about it for the first time, or, as if *we* are surprised by the empty tomb. Rather, let's presume, with Paul, that we know that the resurrection of our Lord has, in fact, already changed things. Our belief in Jesus has identified us with Him in such a way, that we are changed! We have been given a new position—raised—as well as a new disposition—hearts and minds set on the things that are above!

Our true self—our hearts—are with Christ, enthroned with the power of God. And so, our minds are focused on eternal things, not earthly things. What are the eternal things? Well, Paul tells us in Colossians 3:12–17:

> As *God's* chosen ones, holy and beloved, clothe yourselves with *compassion, kindness, humility, meekness,* and *patience.* Bear with one another, and, if anyone has a complaint against another, *forgive* each other; just as the Lord has forgiven you, so you also must forgive. Above all clothe yourselves with *love,* which binds everything together in perfect *harmony.* And let the *peace* of Christ rule in your hearts, to which indeed you were called in the one Body. And *be thankful.* Let the word of Christ dwell in you

richly; teach and admonish one another in all *wisdom*, and with *gratitude* in your hearts sing psalms, hymns, and spiritual songs to God. And *whatever you do*, in word or deed, do everything in the name of the Lord Jesus, giving thanks to God the Father through Him! (Emphasis mine.)

But why should we, the faithful, no longer bother with earthly things? Read what Paul said: "You have died!" (Colossians 3:3). *We* are resurrection people. Our life has an eternal quality to it now: divine, elevated, above the world! *We* are no longer *of* this world even though we are still *in* this world. Our attitude, then, toward the things of earth should be that, ultimately, they are *not* the sources of meaning in our lives; they are dispensable; they are not essential to our true purpose anymore. And so, the "gratitude in our hearts" compels us to give ourselves more and more to God's divine purposes, all for the sake of His glory!

"When Christ, who is our life, appears, then you also will appear with Him in glory!" (Colossians 3:4). This is our future, our eternal future—being with Him … in glory!

Let us glorify the Lord!

The Road of Grace

Now that we have been justified by his blood,
we will be saved through him from the wrath of God.
For if, while we were enemies,
we were reconciled to God through the death of his Son,
much more surely, having been reconciled,
will we be saved by his life.
But more than that,
we even boast in God through our Lord Jesus Christ,
through whom we have now received reconciliation.
Therefore, just as sin came into the world through one man,
and death came through sin,
and so death spread to all because all have sinned
—sin was indeed in the world before the law,
but sin is not reckoned when there is no law.
Yet death exercised dominion from Adam to Moses,
even over those whose sins were not like the transgression of Adam,
who is a type of the one who was to come.

—ROMANS 5:9B-6:4

In First Corinthians 15:22, Paul said: "As in Adam all die, so in Christ all will be made alive!" Which road do you want to take? Are you in Adam, or are you in Christ?

Romans 5:12–14 reads almost as if Paul has created a chart with two columns. At the head of one column is the name Adam. At the head of the other is Christ. Under Adam are listed the words sin, death, trespass, condemnation, and disobedience. Under Christ are listed the words grace, life, gift, one act of Righteousness, justification, obedience. Adam's list is law. Christ's list is grace.

Are you in Adam, or are you in Christ?

In Romans 5:21, Paul says: "Just as sin reigned in death, so also grace might reign through righteousness to bring eternal life through Jesus

Christ." The reign of grace leads us up the Road of Grace. We want to take the road, the column, of Christ. We want to be in Christ. A believer is in Christ.

Back up. Verse 9 says: "Since we have now been justified by His Blood, how much more shall we be saved from God's wrath through Him!" This is true because of what Paul said in verse 8: "God demonstrates His love for us in this: While we were still sinners, Christ died for us!"

How much more …! Grace! Love freely given! Undeserved. Unmerited. Abundant! How much more shall we be saved from God's wrath through Jesus Christ! Through what Jesus has done by accepting the pain of my guilt and the shame of my sin in His Body as He suffered His anguish in the Garden; His arrest, His abuse, and His trial; and His death on the cross. The punishment I deserved, he endured! "He was wounded for our transgressions, crushed for our iniquities, upon Him was the punishment that made us whole, and by His bruises we are healed. All we like sheep have gone astray; we have all turned to our own way; and the Lord has laid on Him the iniquity of us all!" (Isaiah 53:5–6).

God's grace in Christ is abundant! How blessed we are to experience it over and over, again and again!

"What shall we say then? Shall we go on sinning so that grace may increase?" (Romans 6:1). There is this worldly notion that, since our sins are forgiven over and over, it doesn't matter what we do. If we sinned again, we'd just keep getting forgiven anyway, wouldn't we? After all, Jesus is in the business of forgiveness! So go ahead and sin. In fact, keep on sinning, and grace will increase! Right?

By no means! Don't we experience God's grace in Jesus Christ in such a way that we turned and repented? Were we not saved *from* something? Didn't we accept a lifeline to be drawn aboard a sturdy ship? How foolish to say we should go back to our old sinking boat to be thrown a lifeline again. How foolish to continue to make holes in our raft after they've just been mended!

"By no means! We died to sin! How can we live in it any longer?" (6:2). Weren't we changed? By grace didn't we experience being made right with God? If we were made right, why should we ever want to do wrong? To do so would be to mock the gift that we've been given. No! We died to sin!

Paul calls the sacrament of baptism to mind. "Don't you know that all of us who were Baptized into Christ Jesus were Baptized into His Death? We were therefore buried with Him … in order that, just as Christ was raised from the dead through the glory of the Father, we too might walk in newness of life!" (6:3–4).

We don't go back to our old life! Christ has given a new life. In Christ we have eternal life! In Adam, death.

Now some hear the words about baptism, and, being buried and then being raised, as an affirmation of emersion baptism—going under the water (buried), and then being lifted up from the water (being raised). And they believe, therefore, that only a believer's baptism is true baptism. And infant baptism does not comply with these words. But this passage goes so much deeper than the issue of what method best serves this symbolic cleansing.

To be baptized is to be identified with Christ. To be in Christ. To claim to be in Christ! When an infant is baptized, the parents are saying that they promise to raise the child in Christ, and that, at some time, that child will *confirm* for themselves the promise of their baptism. But most importantly, to be baptized into Christ is to be identified with Christ. Therefore, we accept a certain posture toward sin. "We died to sin!"

Now, I have never been dead. But I am afflicted with the disease of mortality. The good news is that I am alive in the Spirit of Christ. I believe in Jesus. And Jesus said: "I am the resurrection and the Life, they who believe in me will live, even though they die! And whoever lives and believes in me shall never die!" (John 11:25–26). Life!

But "sin, when it is full grown, gives birth to death!" (James 1:15). "The wages of sin is death … but the free gift of God is eternal life in Christ Jesus our Lord!" (Romans 6:23).

Let's finish this meditation with the word form First Corinthians: "As in Adam all die, so in Christ all will be made alive!" (15:22).

Are you in Adam or are you in Christ? How can you show it?

A Death like His

Do you not know that all of us who have been baptized into Christ
were baptized into his death?
Therefore we have been buried with him by baptism into his death,
so that, just as Christ was raised from the dead by the glory of the Father,
so we too might walk in newness of life.
For If we have been united with him in a death like his,
we will certainly be united with him in a resurrection like his.
We know that our old self was crucified with him
so that the body of sin might be destroyed,
and we might no longer be enslaved to sin.
For whoever has died is freed from sin.
But if we have died with Christ, we believe that we will also live with him.
We know that Christ, being raised from the dead,
will never die again;
death no longer has dominion over him.
The death he died, he died to sin, once for all;
but the life he lives, he lives to God.
So you also must consider yourselves dead to sin
and alive to God in Christ Jesus.
Therefore, do not let sin exercise dominion in your mortal bodies,
to make you obey their passions.
No longer present your members to sin as instruments of wickedness,
but present yourselves to God
as those who have been brought from death to life,
and present your members to God as instruments of righteousness.
For sin will have no dominion over you,
since you were not under law but under grace.

—ROMANS 6:3–14

In 1969, Peter Townsend and the rock group The Who came out with the "rock opera" *Tommy*. It was a satirical portrayal of a messiah cult. As a young boy, Tommy is shocked into a catatonic state of "unknowing." He seems unable to see, hear, or speak. All he becomes able to say is, "See me; feel me; touch me; heal me." By chance, however, he discovers pinball! He becomes the Pinball Wizard. He plays with no distractions. He can't hear any buzzes or bells. He sees no game lights flashing. He plays by sense of smell!

A doctor suggests that, since there's really nothing wrong with his senses, he needs something to shock him out of his "isolation." This happens abruptly when he goes to a mirror and is enthralled by his own reflection. His mother becomes angry in her frustration with her son. And when she smashes the mirror, Tommy is awakened and healed.

Somehow, he becomes a messiah figure, and his followers all have to play pinball. But to truly be Tommy's disciples, they must become deaf, dumb, and blind. They put in earplugs, their mouths are corked, and they must wear eyeshades through which they cannot see.

Finally, a few pinball disciples take off these gimmicks and the chant begins: "We're not gonna take it." Tommy is rejected and abandoned. When all have deserted him, he is last seen alone, saying, "See me, feel me, touch me, heal me."

So many messiah cults are full of disciples who truly believe that by following the disciplines and lifestyles of the charismatic leader, they will find the same awakening and healing their leader once found. Being a believer is a matter of identifying so strongly with the one in whom you believe that their experience seems to become your experience. Compare it to "your" team winning the Super Bowl, or, the World Series, or your favorite player winning at Wimbledon. Don't we claim victory at their success. Even though we never really scored, we will pat each other on the back, saying, "We won!" Belief can convince us, move us, inspire us to understand the Lord as having truly died for us, and having truly raised us. But it even sounds a bit cultish when Paul says in the Letter to the Romans (6:5), "If we have been united with him in a death like his, we will certainly be united with him in a resurrection like his," speaking of the death and resurrection of Jesus Christ.

But there is a difference, We need to ask ourselves (and Paul) what does he mean by this idea?

There were two men who were united with Jesus in a death like his: they were criminals crucified to His left and to His right (Luke 23:32). But followers of Christ have never actually chosen to be crucified to experience a resurrection.

"One of the criminals who were hanged there kept deriding him and saying, 'Are you not the Messiah? Save yourself and us!'" (23:39) He believed in Jesus. He believed He was the Messiah, but only insofar as He could be saved by Him from his suffering. He missed the whole, true purpose of Jesus.

"Save yourself!" How often are we concerned with saving only ourselves? Did the Good Samaritan save himself? Did the poor widow, giving her penny, save herself? Was the mission of the seventy to save themselves? No. In each case, each *gave* themselves! We need to face the reality that if all we want to do is save ourselves, then our faith is not Christian! Always keep in mind that "as you did it to one of the least of these … you did it unto me" (Matthew 25:40). We are supposed to be faithful by being concerned with the needs of others as if they were Jesus Christ Himself!

The second criminal recognized more in Jesus, and he was promised Paradise! (Luke 23:40–42) But it was not because he was crucified with (like) Christ; it was because he put his trust in Him. In Matthew 16, Jesus said, "Those who want to save their life will lose it, and those who lose their life for my sake will find it" (Matthew 16:25).

In Isaiah 51, the prophet called the people to listen: "Look to Abraham your father and to Sarah who bore you, for he was but one when I called him, but I blessed him and made him many" (51:2).

"Listen to me, my people, and give heed to me, my nation; for a teaching will go out from me, and my justice for a light to the peoples. I will bring near my deliverance swiftly, my salvation has gone out and my arms will rule the peoples; the coastlands wait for me, and for my arm they hope. Lift up your eyes to the heavens, and look at the earth beneath; for the heavens will vanish like smoke, the earth will wear out like a garment, and those who live on it will die like gnats; but my salvation will be forever, and my deliverance will never be ended" (vv. 4–6).

If we all stopped at our own salvation and didn't give ourselves at all to the purposes of God, saving grace would be unknown to generations yet to come. "But my deliverance will be forever, and my salvation to all generations." (51:8) Isaiah wants the people to be "a light to the nations!" (Isaiah 42:6). And our new life in Christ changes us from darkness to light!

"If we have been united with him in a death like his, we will certainly be united with him in a resurrection like his." (Romans 6:5)

What does Paul mean? Look at the very next thing he says as he talks about the "old self."

"We know that our old self has been crucified with him so that the body of sin might be destroyed, and we might no longer be enslaved to sin" (v. 6). By faith we identify with Christ to the degree that we sense that what has happened to Him changes *our own* reality. "The death he died, he died to sin, once for all, but the life he lives, he lives to God. So you must consider yourself dead to sin and alive to God in Christ Jesus" (v. 11). We are to "present ourselves to God as those who have been brought from death to life" (v. 13). All this because we are "under grace" (v. 14). Our baptism is the sign of our identity in Christ. It celebrates a promise we accept. And as we identify with our Lord, we can begin to *consider* His grace—He died to save us … from sin, for eternity—the resurrection like His.

"Therefore we have been buried with him by baptism into his death, so that, just as Christ was raised from the dead by the glory of the Father, so we too might walk in newness of life" (Romans 6:4).

We are not literally *buried* with Jesus, but we embrace His promise to such a degree that we can "consider" His act as our death to sin, and, therefore our aliveness to God. Resurrection!

Crucifixion, the cross, is our point of reference. It was on the cross that Jesus made the saving sacrifice that defeats sin in our lives. Therefore, the cross is a sign of sacrifice … self-sacrifice, self-giving. And Jesus calls us all to "take up a cross and follow" (Matthew 16:24). We are to take up the spirit of self-sacrifice. When we do, we will be "united with him in a death like his!"

Buried with Him

Therefore we have been buried with him by baptism into death,
that, just as Christ was raised from the dead by the glory of the Father,
so we might walk in newness of life.

—ROMANS 6:4

A woman I came to know very well in one of the churches I have served, lost her husband to cancer before their marriage was three years old. They had been very much in love, and her spirit was so broken that she felt that, as she put it, "My heart was buried with him." "Buried with him." She had given him her heart through her love and devotion to him. She loved him so much that, in many ways, he was everything to her. He was her life.

At first, she wondered how she could go on. She had no children, and so in her grief, she felt as though she had nothing to live for. She continued to work, functioning rather mechanically —she described it as "like a zombie"—because, she said, "My heart just wasn't in it." After all, her heart was buried with her husband.

About a year had passed, and though things did get better, and that zombie-like numbness faded away enough for her smile to return sometimes, she still couldn't begin dating again, even though her friends encouraged her, and she'd had a few offers. She always said no, because her "heart just wasn't in it."

Our baptism is an outward and visible sign of an inward and spiritual grace. It expresses our love and devotion to Jesus Christ. In a sense, it is an act that indicates that we have given Him our hearts. Jesus Christ becomes everything to us. He becomes our life. So, in a spiritual sense, we invest ourselves in Jesus Christ in such a way that our identity, who we are, what we live for, and why we live, is in Him.

This becomes so true for us spiritually that we begin to recognize His suffering on the cross as our suffering for sin; His death is the death of our old self, and His resurrection is our new life. Often, we recognize the resurrection of Christ merely as the basis for our belief in Jesus. His resurrection proves who He is. It proves that He is the son of God. It proves that He had the power —power over death, and power to defeat Satan. It proves His innocence, and therefore that His death on the cross was the penalty paid for *our* sins—the sins of the whole world. And for those who might not accept the truth of the resurrection, their only proof would be a dead body. And the body of Christ has never been found, except in its new form, for the church has become the Body of Christ, revealing the power of the resurrection in the new life of His believers, in the discipleship of His followers, and in the glorious grace that has continued for twenty centuries by the working of His Holy Spirit.

We were buried with Him by baptism. It is not a literal burial, nor is this image an indication that Paul believed that baptism must be done by immersion only. Baptism is a symbolic act, and however it may be done, it represents our identification with, and our initiation into, the life of Christ.

Initiation. We are initiated into His death as well. We were buried with Him by baptism into His death. Baptism is not just a ceremony that admits someone into the fellowship of a spiritual club. It is more of an installation. Some have described it as our ordination into the servant-fellowship of Christ. We vow to invest ourselves in Him in such a way as to do the things He did, to walk His walk and live His life to the best of our ability. Ordination is a "setting apart." We are set apart from the world for a purpose different than the world's agenda.

And so, our baptism brings us into the purpose of Christ's death—which is the forgiveness of sin and the reconciliation of the world. Paul put it this way in 2 Corinthians 5:14–20a:

> For the love of Christ controls us, because we are convinced that one has died for all; therefore, all have died. And He died for all, that those who live might live no longer for themselves but for Him who for their sake died and was raised. From now on, therefore, we regard

no one from a human point of view; even though we once regarded Christ from a human point of view, we regard Him thus no longer. Therefore, if anyone is in Christ, they are a new creation; the old has passed away, behold, the new has come. All this is from God, who through Christ reconciled us to Himself and gave us the ministry of reconciliation; that is, in Christ God was reconciling the world to Himself, not counting their trespasses against them, and entrusting to us the message of reconciliation. So we are ambassadors for Christ, God making His appeal through us.

We were buried, therefore, with Him by baptism into death, so that as Christ was raised from the dead by the glory of the Father, we too might walk in newness of life. In Romans 6:10–11, Paul says: "The death He died, He died to sin, once for all; but the life He lives, He lives to God. So you also must consider yourselves dead to sin and alive to God in Christ Jesus." The death we die through the symbolic act of our baptism is a death to sin. Notice it is not the death *of* sin. If we are in this mortal flesh, temptations will come to challenge and prove the grace of our baptism. But we should consider ourselves as having a new status, with a new perspective, standing in a new position before God. "From now on, we regard no one from a human point of view" (2 Corinthians 5:16). Identifying with Christ, we are not just buried with Him; we are raised to new life!

That woman whose husband died before they had been married three years found her heart again. She met another young man who loved her. She said that his love resurrected her heart. And, when I began to know her, she had enjoyed over forty years of marriage and had now already been a widow again for many years. But this time, she did not let her heart get buried with her second husband. She never remarried, but her heart was very alive. She was a woman of great compassion and a church member with great zeal. Her spirit was one that was always kind and gracious, and her attitude was always cheerful. The Spirit of Jesus Christ was very alive in her, and she became a blessing to me, and to many others.

Identifying with Christ, we are not just buried with Him; we are raised to new life. "For if we have been united with Him in a death like His, we shall certainly be united with Him in a resurrection like His!" (Romans 6:5). We are blessed both in Christ's death and in His resurrection!

A Resurrection like His

If we have been united with Him in a death like His,
we shall certainly be united with Him in a resurrection like His.

—ROMANS 6:5

The resurrection of Christ is the central conviction of the Christian faith. Upon His rising from the dead hinges the power of all our hope for ourselves. Two criteria used throughout the New Testament establish Jesus as the Messiah, the Savior. First is the fulfillment of prophecy. And Jesus fulfilled dozens of prophetic visions from the Hebrew scriptures. The second criterion is the resurrection. And although we are not saved by His resurrection but by His death, (for His resurrection proves the grace of God experienced in His death), the faith we have, our beliefs, identify us with Jesus Christ in such a way that we can say with Paul: "If we have been united with Him in a death like His, we shall certainly be united with Him in a resurrection like His" (Romans 6:5). And Paul said, in 1 Corinthians 5:17: "If anyone is in Christ, they are a new creation." And we all know what Paul said in Galatians 2:20: "I have been crucified with Christ; it is no longer I who live, but Christ who lives in me."

But what is it that happens to us after we die? How are we raised?

Apart from what will happen at the miraculous Final Judgment portrayed with the visionary images of Christ's Second Coming, it seems that there must be something that happens even now, because we do not believe in a "waiting place" of some sort, and we want to understand that our loved ones are more than just "dead" right now. Paul even suggests that today, while we are yet alive, we should "consider ourselves dead to sin and alive to God in Christ Jesus" (Romans 6:11).

Sometimes, the question is not always How? but When? I don't want to speculate on the "end of time," but I would want to share some of the understanding I have about this issue. First, I believe that God, from the perspective of eternity, does not wait. Eternity is where there is no "time" as we understand it. In eternity, everything "happens" in such a way that nothing is missed. "One day is as a thousand years …" Likewise, everything that "happens" happens in one great constant "now," "And a thousand years is one day" (2 Peter 3:8). Therefore, from this perspective of eternity, God receives into His eternal kingdom those who have been faithful, I believe, at the moment of their death. Everyone's Final Judgment, from the human point of view, is happening yesterday, today, and tomorrow. From the eternal point of view, it will have happened only once.

The question of *how* we are raised, what is it that happens to us, is a little bit harder.

In 1 Corinthians chapter 15, it seems that Paul was trying to answer the very same questions. Paul uses the metaphor of the seed dying to give life to the shoots and roots. His ultimate point, however, is that we are "raised a spiritual body" (v. 44). And he says, "Just as we have borne the image of the man of dust, we shall also bear the image of the man of heaven" (v. 49) Paul even goes so far as to say that "flesh and blood cannot inherit the Kingdom of God, nor does the perishable inherit the imperishable" (v. 50). And finally, he says: "Lo, I tell you a mystery: We shall not all sleep, but we shall all be changed" (v. 51). In his Letter to the Philippians, Paul also says that Jesus Christ "will change our lowly body to be like His glorious Body" (3:21).

I believe that, since it is not our flesh and blood that is raised, it is our spirit. It is not our "outer nature" that is "wasting away" but our "inner nature," which is "being renewed every day" (2 Corinthians 4:16). Paul here suggests the invisibility (from the human point of view) of things that are eternal: "We look not to the things that are seen, but to the things that are unseen; for the things that are seen are transient (only temporary), but the things that are unseen are eternal" (4:18).

But will we continue to be unique? Will we continue to have our own recognizable personality? The answer is yes! We do not get lost as some Eastern religions describe it, becoming like a single drop of water returning to some vast sea. We, who we truly are, continue to exist. I have known people who have even wondered if those they have loved, who died long ago, will be able to "recognize" them, after all the changes they have gone through as they aged. Again, know that this question comes from the human point of view. But Paul suggests: "From now on, we regard no one from a human point of view ... If anyone is in Christ, they are a new creation" (2 Corinthians 5:16–17) First, I believe that, in eternal life, there will be no such thing as *not* recognizing one another—"Grace was given to each of us according to the measure of Christ's gift." Secondly, our God is a knowing God. "Thou knowest when I sit down and when I rise up. Thou didst knit me together in my mother's womb" (Psalm 139:2, 13). Besides this, I understand God's eternal kingdom as reflecting a perfect oneness that is to begin here and now—"There is one Body and one Spirit, One Lord, one faith, one Baptism, one God and Father of us all, who is above all and through all and in all" (Ephesians 4:4–6). Even now we are to see ourselves as "members of one another" (Ephesians 4:25). Recognition will be instant and automatic.

After we die, we do *not* become "angels." Angels are already part of God's divine order of creation. Nothing scriptural even suggests that a human being becomes an angel. People, all through time, have propagated this illusion to foster a sense of assurance or ease in their children when, from a human point of view, we cannot know exactly what we become. We were "made a little less than angels" (Psalm 8:5). Jesus himself said that "in the resurrection they neither marry nor are given in marriage, but are like angels in heaven" (Matthew 22:30). We may be *like* angels, in that we, in our eternal state will not have a corporeal existence, but we do not become angels.

After we die, we do not become "ghosts" either, or some nearly transparent but visible hologram-like "being" that is able to return to the living world and "exist" in some fashion. There may be something very real to the experience people have that gives them a sense of "presence" about a lost loved one, but the belief in "ghosts" or "spirits of the dead" being present or able to be summoned is a satanic and therefore "false" doctrine.

And finally, we do not become reincarnated! We are resurrected! The idea of reincarnation is not Christian at all and cannot fit in to Christian theology at all. It is a philosophy that does seem to propagate the sense of a continuation after death, as does the resurrection, but it seems to deny the redeeming grace of Jesus Christ in the cross and the mercifulness of

God's judgment. Christian doctrine offers either eternal life or eternal death for the soul. To suggest that someone must return to a new form of life, or "existence," to "do better," or to make up for errors in their lifetime smacks of works-righteousness and denies that we are "saved only by faith" (Romans 1:17). And likewise, to suggest that someone was not "good enough" to go to heaven denies both the grace and the judgment of God. And we Christians believe that God is the only judge! Hebrews 9:27 says: "It is appointed for mortals to die once, and then comes judgment."

After we die, we become "saints"—the holy. God raises us to "perfection" (Hebrews 6:1; Philippians 3:2). We become "one in the Spirit" with Christ in eternity. Eternal life is a "new life in Christ." We are "changed." We are "a new creation." Today we are to live in such a way that we "may gain Christ and be found in Him not having a righteousness of our own …, but that which is through faith in Christ, the righteousness from God that depends on faith; that I may know Him and the power of His resurrection, and may share in His sufferings, becoming like Him in His death, that if possible I may attain the resurrection of the dead" (Philippians 3:8–11).

I cannot say what we become, but I can say that we will be changed. I cannot say exactly *how* we are changed, but I can say we are becoming a new creation. And I don't know exactly what it will be like, but it will be eternal!

That eternity begins with our being united with Jesus in a death like His. Listen to what Paul says following verse 5 in Romans 6: "We know that our old self was crucified with Him so that the sinful body might be destroyed, and we might no longer be enslaved to sin. For they who have died are freed from sin. But if we have died with Christ, we believe that we shall also live with Him. For we know that Christ being raised from the dead will never die again; death no longer has dominion over Him. The death he died He died to sin, once for all, but the life He lives He lives to God. So you also must consider yourselves dead to sin and alive to God in Christ Jesus!" (Romans 6:7–11).

Just remember, "If anyone is in Christ, they are a new creation!" (2 Corinthians 5:17). Enter into Christ, and you enter into life. Life eternal!

Now That We Are Reconciled

While we were still weak,
at the right time Christ died for the ungodly.
Indeed, rarely will anyone die for a righteous person—
though perhaps for a good person someone might actually dare to die.
But God proves his love for us in that
while we were sinners Christ died for us.
Much more surely then, now that we have been justified by his blood,
will we be saved through him from the wrath of God.
For if while we were enemies,
we were reconciled to God through the death of his Son,
much more surely, having been reconciled,
will we be saved by his life.
But more than that,
we even boast in God through our Lord Jesus Christ,
through whom we have now received reconciliation.
—Romans 5:6–11

"While we were still weak …"
"While we were yet sinners …"
"While we were enemies …"

Tony Campolo, a Christian author and very intense public speaker, tells a story about a friend of his, a woman, who, long ago, had been a fifth-grade teacher. Her name is Jean Thomson. And the story he tells is about a student named Teddy Stollard. Miss Thomson was especially known for the big red marks she loved to put next to the wrong answers on the papers her students turned in. But she didn't know … She didn't know that for one boy those marks always hurt. And she should have known better, Campolo said, because Teddy's record included comments from his previous teachers, and she could have learned something about his past.

In first grade, his teacher had written: "Teddy shows great promise as a student, even though his home time is difficult." In second grade, his teacher wrote: "Teddy is doing well, but his mother has terminal cancer and his father shows little interest in Teddy's work. In third grade, the teacher wrote. "Teddy's having trouble in school. His mother died this year!"

By fifth grade, Teddy always slouched at his desk. He didn't have clean clothes on very often, and his hair was always musty and unkempt. He never spoke with much more than monosyllabic answers. And he just didn't seem to care. Every big, bold red mark Miss Thomson gave him made him care less and less. It seemed, to her, like he was headed for little more than problems down the road.

Christmastime came, and most of the students brought neatly wrapped little presents for Miss Thomson and placed them on her desk. One was a package from Teddy. She was surprised he even brought something. It was wrapped poorly in brown paper, taped together with masking tape, and on it, written in dull crayon, it said, "To Miss Thompson, from Teddy S."

When, in front of all the children, she opened his package, out fell a rhinestone bracelet that was missing many stones and a near empty bottle of cheap perfume. All the kids chuckled, but Miss Thomson had enough of the spirit of Christmas and the presence of mind to keep everyone from making Teddy feel ashamed of his gift. She snapped on the bracelet right away and dabbed a bit of the perfume on her wrist. She let everyone know it was a pleasant scent by holding out her wrist to some of the closest students saying, "Doesn't that smell nice?"

At the end of the day, all the students left. Later, while Miss Thomson was bagging all her gifts, Teddy Stollard came back into the room with a warm smile for Miss Thomson. And he said, "Miss Thomson, all day today you smelled just like my mother used to smell. Thanks for liking the perfume," Then off he ran. At that moment, Jean Thomson fell to her knees and cried until she had no more tears. She was changed. What she soon found out was that Teddy was changed too.

Her kindness that day had, in some way, resurrected Teddy's mother for him. And his appreciation, his witness, resurrected something in her.

She was no longer just a teacher of math and language and history. She was a teacher of students. And Teddy was no longer just someone who earned a grade from her, but a child who was coming to learn from her. The whole atmosphere of her classroom had changed. By the end of the school year, Teddy had caught up and was even ahead of some students.

Many years passed, and she never heard from him until she got a simple letter from him in the mail: "Dear Miss Thompson, I will be graduating from high school in a few days. And I just wanted you to know. Thanks for being my teacher." About four years later, another letter came from Teddy: "Dear Miss Thomson, I will be graduating from college in a few days, third in my class! Just wanted you to know." And about another four years later, Miss Thomson had retired, but she got another letter. "Dear Miss Thomson, By the time you get this letter, I will officially be Doctor Theodore Stollard! Dad died last year. In a few months. I'll be getting married to wonderful woman. I'd like to ask you a favor. Could you come to my wedding and sit in the place where my mother would have sat?"

She did. Nowadays, Miss Thomson, who was there when Teddy needed someone, but who, now, had no family, is taken care of by Ted Stollard. What goes around comes around! Even blessings! Especially blessings!

"If … we are reconciled … how much more will we be saved by his life!" (Romans 6:10).

And, "While we were still weak at the right time, Christ died for the ungodly. God shows his love for us in that, while we were yet sinners, Christ died for us. Since, therefore, we are now justified by his blood, much more shall we be saved by him from the wrath of God. For if, while we were enemies we were reconciled to God by the death of his son, much more, now that we are reconciled, shall we be saved by his life" (Romans 6:6–10).

Much more … The resurrection is so much more than just a miracle having to do with Jesus Christ. Because he is alive, we have so much more than just freedom from sin. We have so much more than just a hope in life after death. We have so much more than just grace to overcome our difficult days. We have a power to change! Even though something in us may die, there is a power that gives us life. And that life is much more than a casual existence. It is much more than what our simple celebrations reveal. That life is an ecstasy that fills us with passion. It's as if the rapture of the love we had at first was revived. And now we can let it carry us away. We *should* let it carry us away.

Much more, now that we have been reconciled, shall we be saved by his life! Saved from a commonness, from an ordinariness. We are raised by the realization that a faith in Jesus Christ is nothing casual. We are raised from a dead and dying existence. This life is much more that we seem to treat it. It's like holding lightning. It's like carrying fire. It is glorious! Don't you feel it? Don't you realize?

It changes us! Yes, while we were still weak, while we were still sinners, while we were enemies, Christ died for us! He died to reconcile us to God; to give us strength, to give us holiness, to give us friendship, to give us peace and hope and love! But now, *now* that we are reconciled to God by the death of his son, much more, now that we are reconciled; shall we be saved by his life." His resurrected, unconquerable, everlasting life!

How much does the grace of God really mean to you? Whatever it may mean to you, it is much more!

On the Mountain

Six days later,
Jesus took with him Peter and James and his brother John
and led them up a high mountain, by themselves.
And he was transfigured before them,
and his face shone like the sun, and his clothes became dazzling white.
Suddenly there appeared to them Moses and Elijah, talking with him.
Then Peter said to Jesus,
"Lord, it is good for us to be here;
if you wish, I will make three dwellings here,
one for you, one for Moses, and one for Elijah."
While he was still speaking,
suddenly a bright cloud overshadowed them,
and from the cloud a voice said,
"This is my Son, the Beloved,
with him I am well pleased;
listen to him!"
When the disciples heard this, they fell to the ground
and were overcome by fear.
But Jesus came and touched them,
saying, "Get up and do not be afraid."
And when they looked up, they saw no one except Jesus himself alone.

–MATTHEW 17:1–8

A family of four on vacation was hiking up the mountainside somewhere in Colorado. Their path supposedly led to an isolated but very picturesque lake high above the roadside parking area they had left nearly an hour before. The steep and rocky path proved to be exactly the sort of challenge the teenage boys were looking for. But after this much upward struggling with the constantly unpredictable footing and the shortness of breath brought on by their increasing altitude, they all collapsed on a log by the path in discouragement.

In less than a minute, a group of hikers approached from above already on their way down. One of them noticed the look of disenchantment on the faces of the family resting on the log and said, "Don't give up now! It's beautiful up there! It's worth every step you take!"

The man's words were like a shot of adrenalin to their tired bodies. In another minute, they were forging ahead, glad to be closing in on the end of their climb, but their gladness was a thousand times greater when they saw the splendor to which the path had led. The view from the top was, indeed, magnificent. The glorious view spanned out for miles and miles on the nice crisp day. They breathed deeply, and the air seemed fresher; the water tasted sweeter than any they had ever sipped before. The father even said he felt younger after drinking it. And everyone agreed when the mother said that "after seeing this, nothing can ever be the same!"

On the Mountain!

There is something that we call a mountaintop experience. When I was in college, I coined the phrase, "On the mountain!" for some of us as a sort of inelegant description of feeling good, or great. The words even began to be used by everyone who knew me, as a sort of greeting. The word "mountainous" became the redundant adjective for many of my friends. "How was your test?" "Mountainous!" "How was the party?" "Mountainous!

"Look at her, man. Isn't she mountainous?" I guess that nowadays the overused word is *awesome*. But I felt quite *mountainous* when, one day, I heard a table of girls in the cafeteria, most of whom I didn't even know yet, call out to us as my roommate and I walked by leaving after dinner and said, "On the mountain!"

It's sort of like saying, "I wish for you the feeling of being on the mountain!"

One of the girls said to the three who had called out, "What does that mean?" And I just told her that "you can't get much higher than the mountaintop. Want me to show you?" There is a thrill, an excitement, an awe about having climbed above the world and looked down. It's almost like being able to imagine the view that God might have.

On the mountain!

God was said to be on the mountain when Moses went up to see the burning bush, and when he received the Ten Commandments of the Covenant Law. God had descended to the top of Mount Sinai in a fire, and the smoke from it went up like the smoke of a kiln! (Exodus 19:18). And "the appearance of the Lord was like a devouring fire" (24:17). "And Moses was on the mountain forty days and forty nights" (v. 18).

On the mountain! *In the presence of God and the power of God!*

Peter, James, and John followed Jesus "up a high mountain." And Jesus was transfigured before them. It was Jesus's divine nature that they witnessed. And in the awesomeness of His eternal splendor, they could see both Moses and Elijah. But were they really there? Or was it just Jesus that they saw, and what Moses and Elijah stood for was a part of what they experienced in Christ? Moses represents the law, and Elijah the prophets. All of it together, revealed to Peter, James, and John, without a doubt, that they beheld in Jesus the power of God. I believe Moses and Elijah could have been present, since, by the power of God, Jesus was able to transcend time and experience their company.

We did not follow cleverly devised myths
when we made known to you the power and coming of our Lord Jesus Christ,
but we had been eyewitnesses of his majesty.
For we received honor and glory from God the Father
when that voice was conveyed to him by the Majestic Glory saying,
"This is my Son, my Beloved, with whom I am well pleased."
We ourselves heard this voice come from heaven,
while we ourselves were with him on the holy mountain.

—2 PETER 1:16–18

In those mountainous experiences an assurance comes that tells the heart that there is something more, something great, something so glorious and far beyond our normal grasp that we can't help but want to know it more, to experience it again and again.

But what do we do with those mountaintop experiences? What happens to us when we leave them behind? A great guru was asked why he came down from the mountaintop so often, and he said that it was because there were no outhouses up there. As a matter of fact, something always brings us back down to earth eventually. But, for one, this is where life goes on. We ought to live it. We ought to return to it. We can't be on a constant high all the time! Or can we?

We can't come down and just forget that something real happened within us up *there*. And we can't just assume that what we felt is still up *there* somehow when we stop feeling the exhilarating sensations of being on the mountain. It is something within. Something deep inside us that rises, because we don't need to be at the top of a real mountain to feel that "on the mountain" feeling. What happens to our mountaintop experiences? Well, like the hiker on the way down, we must be able to say to others, "Don't give up!" The transformation we experience can be like a calling. The beauty is not to be kept hidden but exposed. The truth is not to be kept a secret but revealed.

Let me suggest that the church is a sort of mountain. When we take our eyes off the goal, off of Jesus Christ and his purpose for us, the climb becomes tiresome. But the promised splendor of the prize turns the difficult path into little steppingstones, for nothing can compare to what God has prepared for us. And then, for me, being a part of the church is being *on the mountain*! And it's like being surrounded by all these mountainous people! Don't keep it to yourself; let others know how beautiful it is around here and how beautiful it makes you feel inside to have been here, and to think about returning. It's worth every step of the way. And I want every believer to become trail guides: tell others, and show others the way they can go to experience being on the mountain. Don't let anyone get away with saying they've been there, and it's not so great. Whatever it was that prevented them from seeing the splendor on *this* mountain, we can pray that they'll see it now. Seek and you shall find. Ask and it will be given. Maybe they were so exhausted before that they just couldn't see beyond their own pain. Or their mind was stuck in the foothills.

Climb and climb again. Give them a shot of adrenaline. It's worth every step. Don't give up! The resurrection is a mountaintop experience. I believe that the power of God in Jesus Christ that transfigured Him on the mountain was ignited in the tomb at the moment of His rising. I can believe that such a wonderful burst of light may have created the image on the Shroud of Turin. And I believe the power of the resurrection is in the heart of every believer, exuding a beauty so perfect that it can give us a glow. Climb. Strive to rise to the top of the mountain. It's worth every step, every effort of belief, every word of encouragement. Tell the people who need to hear it.

We can feel "resurrection!"

Treasure in Earthen Vessels

We do not proclaim ourselves;
we proclaim Jesus Christ as Lord
and ourselves as your slaves for Jesus' sake.
For it is the God who said,
"Let light shine out of darkness,"
who has shone in our hearts
to give the light of the knowledge of the glory of God
in the face of Jesus Christ.
But we have this treasure in clay jars,
so that it may be made clear that
this extraordinary power belongs to God and does not come from us.
We are afflicted in every way, but not crushed;
perplexed, but not driven to despair;
persecuted, but not forsaken;
struck down, but not destroyed;
always carrying in the body the death of Christ,
so that the life of Jesus may also be made visible in our bodies.

—2 CORINTHIANS 4:5–10

I want to tell you about an old man named Ben Sanford. Ben Sanford was a simple earthen vessel. But it was easy to see the light of God shining in his heart. And sometimes, it's the memories of someone who was a faithful Christian that carries a message better than any meditation full of beautiful theological rhetoric. So let me tell you about old Ben.

He was already eighty-six years old when I first came to know him. And I only knew him a little over a year. But it was easy to discover that Ben Sanford was a special man. He told stories! Old Ben was like the proverbial old-timer with a gleam in his eye and a memory to share. He chewed tobacco, and used to farm, and just about everyone knew who he was. He lived just south of the Milledgeville blacktop on a farm on the road to Sterling, not far from what had once been known as Sanfordville, which didn't exist anymore. But it sure seemed real when old Ben talked about it. You see, there was a mill there in the creek that his great-granddaddy built. It was already old when old Ben was just a boy, but it sure must have been a great place.

One story he told about that mill happened during the peak of the Depression. The mill was going to close because it couldn't make any money in those days. But, on one of the last days, Ben said it was a Friday, a bunch of the men who had just finished work at the end of the day and were cleaning up, washing their hands and arms in the creek, saw something white floating toward them. One guy waded in and fished it out. It was a piece of clothing, a young woman's slip. And interestingly enough, Ben said, someone had written the word "Friday" on the tag inside. Ben said, you should have seen the way a couple of those men tore off upstream hoping to "rescue" the woman who lost her underwear. And then old Ben explained that what they really hoped to find was some young woman bathing in the creek who didn't know her slip had fallen in the water. No one half grown could have drowned in that creek. The only place it ever got deep was right there near the mill.

Well, anyway, they never found any undressed woman they could rescue, but later on, word got out that the young schoolteacher was missing a slip that disappeared from her clothesline. And then Ben said, just like an old-timer, "And to this very day, no one ever found out how I stole that slip and put it in the creek that day."

"But," he went on, "it sure made the Depression a lot easier to take for those boys at the mill. They never stopped telling the story about that 'Friday Slip.' And they always wondered about what it said inside that teacher's underwear on the other days of the week."

Then, when Ben was finished with his story, he'd pick up a can and lean forward and spit. You see, Old Ben always had a chew of tobacco in his mouth. Even in the hospital once, when he had some back trouble, his packet of Red Man and a can were right there on the table beside him. Old Ben admitted to me that he first tried that nasty habit when he was eight years old! That's almost eighty years of chewing! And he still had most of his own teeth! Anyway, if chewing tobacco is a nasty habit, it's the only one he had. But Ben Sanford had a great sense of humor that gave him an aliveness and made him easy to love.

His wife, Frances, told the story once of how he and their son, Benny Jr., had an ongoing wrestling match. Old Ben had said that there would never come a day when Benny would end up on top. But once, when Benny came home well after he was full-grown, and tore off his jacket ready for the big match, old Ben faked a limp around the kitchen table to make his son feel sorry for him. You see, there was no way old Ben Sanford could be beaten. Even if someone disagreed with him, he'd just ask, "Are you going to argue with me?" and if the answer was yes, he would just say, "Well then, there's just no use in talking!"

His son Benny once told me what his father used to tell him when he wasn't so willing to do his chores, he would say, "I can't *make* you do your chores, but I can sure make you wish you had!"

Old Ben Sanford taught the old men's Sunday school class at the Brick Church, (actually, the Elkhorn United Methodist Church), for over fifteen years, and from what I heard, he was quite a preacher. Some of the old men that were in that class still remembered more of the stories old Ben used to tell than most people tell in a lifetime. But Ben was a faithful man. He always had a devotional guide by his favorite chair on the screened-in porch that looked west over the fields to the creek where the old mill used to run.

Ben's last ten days were spent in a still silence in the Sterling hospital after a massive stroke. Each time I saw him there, I'd hold his right hand, and I could still feel his return grip. His eyes would open, and he'd know you were there. And by the time you'd have to leave, and you'd start to let go and pull away, his hold would get just a little tighter. He didn't want to be beaten by the stroke he'd had. He didn't want to be beaten by death. Old Ben was holding on to life.

And, you know, I don't think he ever really let go. Old Ben had a treasure in his heart. There was a light there, a treasure in the earthen vessel of his body that could show that the transcendent power belongs to God. (I like the "earthen vessels" of the King James Version better than the "jars of clay" in the New Revised Standard Version. It just seems more "biblical" to me.) He knew that the power to overcome came from faith. He could have been afflicted in every way but was never crushed. He could have been perplexed but was not driven to despair. He could have been persecuted, but he knew that he would never be forsaken. And even when he was struck down, he was not destroyed (2 Corinthians 4:8–9).

And we can learn from his example. By faith, he was always able to see the brighter side to everything. And because of this, his humor was able to show the lighter side. It takes a little light in the darkness, lightness in the heaviness, of our days to be able to reveal the power of the treasure that's within. But more than anything else, it takes faith. For only by faith can we "carry in the body the death of Jesus, so that the life of Jesus may also be manifested in our bodies" (2 Corinthians 4:10).

We must let ourselves be confronted by the gospel of Christ in such a way that Christ's death and resurrection are more than just events in history, more than just facts, more than just ideas that we accept. Rather, they become a challenge for us today to surrender and be delivered. And we surrender to God to be delivered from evil. We surrender our egos to be delivered from self. We surrender our own self-interests to be delivered from pride. We surrender in love to be delivered from sin. And, like old Ben Sanford, we surrender in joy to be delivered from sadness.

We have this treasure, the treasure of faith—faith in the power of God that overcomes sin through the cross, that overcomes death through the empty tomb, that overcomes evil by the inspiration of the Holy Spirit to do good, and that overcomes the depression, by a little humor. We have this treasure in earthen vessels here and now, before us, within us, around us, and through us. And it shows the transcendent power, the power to overcome, to be afflicted and not crushed, to be perplexed but not driven to despair, to be persecuted but not forsaken, and to be struck down but not defeated. This power belongs to God, but God's power is working, and we are his tools, for we are his!

Relative to the resurrection is the idea of 2 Corinthians 4:10 that "the life of Jesus may also be manifested in our bodies." That's the resurrected life of Christ that shines in our hearts! And it gives us "the light of the knowledge of the glory of God" (2 Corinthians 4:6).

The Padded Cross

A Readers' Theatre skit for five people

I want to know Christ
and the power of his resurrection
and the sharing of his sufferings
by becoming like him in his death,
if somehow I may attain
the resurrection from the dead.

—PHILIPPIANS 3:10–11

The readers:

1. (Standing at the pulpit)
2. and # 3. (Center stage)
4. (Unseen, has a microphone)
5. (Enters later, then leaves)

1. Philippians 3, verse 10: "I want to know Christ …"
2. (*Interrupting, enthusiastic*) Amen to that, brother! I want to know Christ, just like Paul. Jesus Christ, He's my savior. "God so loved the world that He sent His only Son, so that whoever believes in Him shall not perish, but have eternal life!" That's John 3:16. And I believe!
3. You believe!?
2. Yes! (very self-satisfied). I believe Jesus is the Son of God!
3. And that's all you think you need to do? Believe? "Even the demons believe, and it makes them shudder!" That's James 2, verse 19!
2. Even the demons believe?
3. What is it you believe about Jesus?
1. Philippians 3, verse 10—"I want to know Christ, and the power of His resurrection."

2. The resurrection! I believe in the resurrection!

4. There is no resurrection without a death!

2. I believe Jesus died. Yes. He died on a cross!

3. What about that death? What do you know about Christ's death?

2. Well. Oh, yeah … He died for the sins of the whole world!

3. How did He die?

2. Umm. … They crucified Him.

3. On a cross?

2. That's right!

3. What was it Jesus said about crosses before He died?

2. (*pause*) I can't remember.

1. Matthew 16, verse 24—"Then Jesus told His disciples, 'If any want to become my followers, let them deny themselves and take up their crosses and follow me.'"

2. I have to *deny* myself?

4. "Those who lose their life for my sake will find it!" (Matthew 16:25b)

3. And … take up a cross!

2. What does that mean, take up a cross? What kind of cross? I have a little wooden cross on my key-chain. Sometimes people wear a cross on a necklace.

5. (*entering from elsewhere*) Well, here I am, Lord. You said, "Take up your cross," and I'm here to do it. It's not easy, you know, this self-denial thing. I mean to go through it though—yes, sir. I'll bet you wish more people were willing to be a disciple like me. I've counted the cost and surrendered my life, and it's not an easy road. Do you mind if I look over these crosses? I'd kind of like a new one … (*Pause*) I was wondering — are there any that have vinyl padding? I am thinking of attracting others, see. And if I could show them a comfortable cross, I'm sure I could win a lot more. Is there one that's sort of flat so it would fit under my coat? One shouldn't be too obvious. Funny, there doesn't seem to be much choice here—just that coarse, rough wood. I mean, that would hurt. … What's that? It's either one of these or forget the whole thing? Lord, I want to be Your disciple, but life has to have a balance, too. … You don't understand—nobody lives that way today. I mean, being a disciple is challenging and exciting, and I

want to do it, but I do have some rights, you know … Lord? … Lord? Jesus? Now, where do you suppose He went? (exit)

2. I have to take up a *real* cross?

1. Philippians 3, verse 10—"I want to know Christ and the power of the resurrection and the fellowship of His sufferings …"

2. (interrupting urgently) Do I have to *suffer*?

3. Well, you have to take up a cross! You said you wanted to know Christ, just like Paul!

2. Yeah, but … that was because I wanted to know the power of His resurrection!

4. There are many who love the glory of His kingdom, but few who would bear His cross!

2. But Jesus was the Son of God! He is the savior! He *had* to die for our sins!

4. There are many who seek the joy of His salvation, but few who willingly sacrifice their pleasures to find it.

2. What *sacrifice* do I have to make?

1. Philippians 3, verse 10: I want to know Christ and the power of His resurrection and the fellowship of His sufferings … by becoming like Him in His death.

2. Do I have to die like Jesus?

4. There are many who desire His consolation, but few His tribulation!

3. Do you still want to know Christ?

2. I want to know the resurrection!

3. Will you deny yourself and take up a cross?

2. (pause, sorting things out — weighing sacrifice and resurrection, resignedly) Yes, I will take up a cross.

4. There are many who would walk with Christ, but many only hope that the way is smooth and safe.

1. Romans 5, verses 3 through 5: "We rejoice in our sufferings, knowing that suffering produces endurance, and endurance produces character, and character produces hope, and hope does not disappoint us, because God's love has been poured into our hearts through the Holy Spirit."

2. (*very resignedly, with a big sigh*) I will take up a cross. God's love has been poured into my heart! (*now very positively*) I can rejoice in my suffering. I will make sacrifices to know the power of His resurrection!

4. "Come, O blessed of my Father, inherit the kingdom prepared for you from the foundation of the world!"

1. 1. Matthew 25, verse 34. (*Pause, then …*) Philippians 3, verses 10 and 11: "I want to know Christ and the power of His resurrection and the fellowship of His sufferings by becoming like Him in His death, if somehow I may attain the resurrection of the dead."

Pastor: Let us pray: Dear heavenly Father, we come before You today, each with our own trials and sufferings, and our own crosses to bear. We are aware, Lord, that you know what it is like to suffer, and it is not that You wish us pain in our life, but rather, it is through our pain that we can draw nearer to You. Help us, Lord, to recognize Your purpose in our lives and allow our crosses to enable us to become better followers of Your Way. In Jesus's name I pray. Amen.

The Empty Cross

I have been crucified with Christ;
and it is no longer I who live, but Christ who lives in me.
And the life I now live in the flesh
I live by faith in the Son of God, who loved me and gave himself for me.

—GALATIANS 2:19B-20

A peculiar story that goes back to the first century tells about how a youth apprenticed to a carpenter who worked out of a town near Jerusalem came to the Holy City on Easter Sunday to do some trading. It was about midmorning, and the road he took led him past the place where, only two days before, three criminals had been crucified. Since it had been the Feast of the Passover the day before, no one had taken the crosses down yet. No one worked on the Sabbath in Jerusalem, especially at the time of the Passover.

As the boy moved slowly past the crosses, he examined them. He noticed the quality of the cut and the flow of the grain. They were made of strong, solid, fresh wood. The wood that made the crosses could have been used to make good strong walls or ceilings in a home or city building. He himself had fashioned many such beams under the direction of his teacher.

Something drew him to move closer to the cross in the center. He noticed the blood stains where the nails had held the hands and feet of its victim. He saw the ends of the cross beam where a little sap had bled from the wood. He didn't want to touch the cross; it would be unclean because it had touched death. Slowly, he walked around to see the other side, and there, near the foot of the cross he saw … *his* mark! The letters of his name! This was a beam he had prepared! It had been used to crucify some criminal! Carpenters always put their mark on their work. He saw his name carved on that cross, and suddenly a flash of recognition surged within him, and he felt ashamed at such a horrible use of his work. But then, along with his shame, he felt as though a part of him had died with whoever was crucified on that cross! He hoped that no one he knew would ever see that the cross had ever had anything to do with him. But he felt that the whole world must already know. He felt that somehow it was he who had been crucified, because the cross had been hewn by his hand.

Later, when he learned that it was Jesus Christ who had been crucified on that cross, the wound of his shame seemed to reopen. His heart was broken. He felt that his life was draining from him, from the inside. He felt that it was he who had crucified the Messiah. He began to feel the wounds of Jesus, because he had known Jesus, he had heard Jesus. He had believed in Jesus. And so, he had died with Jesus. But after he learned of the resurrection, the feeling returned that, in some way, the part of him that had died with the man who was crucified had needed to die. And now, because of the resurrection, somehow he had been reborn He felt changed. A new man. A man who had died and was raised to new life. And the way the story ends is with another young man coming into the Holy City, passing by the cross, examining it, just as the carpenter's apprentice had done, except when he came to the other side and gazed at the carved markings near the foot of the cross, he saw *his* name there. And then, others, in the very same way, saw their names.

Do you feel that your name is carved into that cross?

Can you say with Paul, "I have been crucified with Christ; it is no longer I who live but Christ who lives in me"?

Do you feel that you have been crucified with Christ? Is Christ living in you? Can you say that "the life I now live in the flesh I live by faith in the Son of God, who loved me and gave himself for me?" Is Jesus Christ set free in your life, or do you hold him captive where he can't get out?

We need the cross! We need that empty cross. A cross, not a crucifix. Not a cross with an image of a dead Christ still nailed to it. He was on the cross less than six hours; a crucifix freezes him there forever. Jesus was taken down and buried. Come to the cross, the bare cross, the empty cross of Christ. For in that image is power.

From Mount Hor they set out by the way to the Red Sea,
to go around the land of Edom;
but the people became impatient on the way.
They spoke against God and against Moses.

"Why have you brought us up out of Egypt to die in the wilderness?
For there is no food and no water,
and we detest this miserable food."
Then the Lord sent poisonous serpents among the people,
and they bit the people, so that many Israelites died.
The people came to Moses and said,
"We have sinned by speaking against the Lord and against you;
pray to the Lord to take away the serpents from among us."
So Moses prayed for the people.
And the Lord said to Moses,
"Make a poisonous serpent, and set it on a pole;
and everyone who is bitten shall look at it and live."
So Moses made a serpent of bronze,
and put it on a pole;
and whenever a serpent bit someone,
that person would look at the serpent of bronze and live.

—NUMBERS 21:4–9

It's a power not unlike the power offered to the Israelites when they gazed toward the bronze serpent on the pole. It's a power that shows the way of overcoming. The Israelites had to journey through a dry, barren wilderness. There was no food, no water, and although God still sustained them by the miraculous daily provision of manna, they complained. And not just about Moses, but about God. And God saw their lack of faith. They were faithful only when things were getting better. A little trial, and they rebelled. They wanted things their way, not God's. And in judgment, God sent a plague of "fiery serpents," or probably poisonous snakes. And when the suffering got worse, they repented. They acknowledged that they had sinned, and they pleaded with Moses, and Moses pleaded with God, and God appointed him to raise up a bronze serpent on a pole for them to look at and be healed.

The serpent on a pole symbol is called a *caduceus*. We often see it at pharmacies. It is a symbol of healing.

The symbol of their judgment became the reminder of their repentance and the power of their ability to overcome. And that's the same power that is the power of the cross. They were healed, not by any magic created by an ornament but by their repentance,

"Death, where is thy sting? The sting of death is sin" (1 Corinthians

15:55–56). "The word of the cross is foolishness to those who are perishing, but to us who are being saved it is the power of God!" (1 Corinthians 1:18).

"Just as Moses lifted up the serpent in the wilderness, so must the son of man be lifted up, that whoever believes in him may have eternal life" (John 3:14–15). There is a power through belief. And religious belief is much more than mere intellectual ascent or acceptance. "When I am lifted up from the earth, I will draw all people to myself" (John 12:32). It is a compelling force.

Forgiveness comes from the cross. Forgiveness is the thing that draws us, that reconciles us to God, and to each other. But there is no forgiveness if there is no repentance, and there is no forgiveness if we do not believe what Jesus has done for us on the cross. In fact, there is no salvation without the cross! Jesus died for us. Jesus died for our sins. Jesus died on a cross. God gave his only Son that whoever believes in Him should not perish.

The power of God is revealed to us in the cross. "When I came to you," Paul said, "I did not come proclaiming to you the testimony of God in lofty words or wisdom for I decided to know nothing among you except Jesus Christ and Him crucified. And I was with you in weakness and in much fear and trembling; and my speech and my message were not in plausible words of wisdom but in demonstration of the Spirit and of power, that your faith might not rest in the wisdom of men, but in the power of God" (1 Corinthians 2:1–5). The power of God!

It's a power that comes through a very humble medium—a cross. An instrument of judgment that has become the reminder of our repentance and the symbol of overcoming. But it reminds us of a power so great, it transcends, overcomes the grave. It is a power so good it defeats and overcomes death. So wonderful it overcomes this life and gives new life. The empty cross becomes very precious to us. So precious that we would coat it with brass. So precious that we would wear it as jewelry. So precious because we want to remember the power that it signifies for our lives. So precious because of what we are given because of it. We are disciples. And the cross reminds us of our calling. "If any one would come after me, let them deny themselves and take up their cross and follow me" (Matthew 16:24).

There's a story, I believe it's from Bunyan's *Pilgrim's Progress*, about two men who were disciples of Jesus. Both were given huge crosses to carry on their journeys through life toward the promised land. Many times they were tempted to shorten the stem of their heavy crosses. One man finally did so, but the other man thought he'd better not. This was the cross God had given him, and this was the cross he knew he must carry. It must not be given up in any way. After many years of journeying, they came within sight of a glorious land. Just the distant view caused the feeling that they were already home. But there was a narrow but incredibly deep chasm they had to cross. The men looked at their crosses. The one who had cut the stem short on his cross could not use it to bridge the gap. But the cross of the other one seemed long enough. He tried it, and it was able to reach across ... just barely. He carefully walked across trying very hard not to look down, and he made it. He made it, thankful that it was able to serve as the bridge necessary to reach the glorious land, thankful that he had not sought an easier way, and thankful for the power that is faith, the power that made him able to bear his cross. The power of the cross.

After reaching the other side, he turned back to watch and encourage his companion when he would cross over. But the cross that had been his cross had disappeared. On his head, he now had a crown. He had exchanged his cross for a crown. The friend could not traverse the chasm on the first man's cross, and his was too short since he had trimmed the stem. It was a sad moment of realization: we cannot reach heaven on another person's faith; we must each have our own faith. We must each learn for ourselves the power of the cross we bear.

The empty cross. It's a symbol of our own death because Christ has died for us. It's a symbol of the death of our sins because Jesus died there in our place. He bore the punishment that we deserved. It's a symbol of death's defeat, because the empty cross reminds us that there was an empty tomb too. It's a symbol of the defeat of and the protection from evil. It's a symbol of the death of selfishness for we are called upon to deny self, to take up our own crosses, and to follow Christ. The cross is a symbol of Grace—Jesus *gave* his life, and he gave us His Spirit. God gave his only Son. It's a symbol of love—God *gave* us His only Son because He loved the world He had made. He loved the life He had given to his image and likeness. The cross is a symbol of belief —whoever believes in the one who died there will not perish, but will have eternal life—it's a symbol for life.

But it's also a symbol of judgment—he who does not believe is condemned already. God help us. Help our church! Help us bear our cross.

The Last Enemy

The last enemy to be defeated is death!
—1 CORINTHIANS 15:26

The battle lines are drawn, The battlefield: our hearts. The enemy looms over us. His weapons are so various and so manifold that he seems unconquerable. What chance do we have before his incredible array of pain-inducing, blood-spilling, heartbreaking means of destruction? How can we defeat death?

Our only weapon is the cross of Christ. We bear it so awkwardly though. It's size and weight make it difficult to wield even in our own defense, let alone in a skirmish against any enemy. Especially this one. But, by clinging to the old rugged cross, we proclaim a resolve, a will, an understanding, a belief that we live in the power of the One who had died having been nailed to its beams.

Jesus Christ is on our side! He fights with us! He fights for us! Not only that, but, in *this* battle, he even dies for us. When the battle against death is raging in my life, Jesus dies when I am wounded.

Jesus is bruised when I am battered. I will be healed and given new life. He will take my place before death strikes in a final effort to end my existence.

In a moment, in the twinkling of an eye, I will be changed; death will be defeated for me, and my Defender will absorb death's final stab. At that moment I will be filled with the conqueror's song: "Death is swallowed up in victory! Death, where is thy victory? O Death, where is thy sting?" (1 Corinthians 15:55). And then, an even greater triumph will come. Jesus, not by fooling death, but by having the very power of life, will be seen rising even ahead of me. Death has no power over Him. Never did! When God raised Jesus from the tomb, Death was subjected to His will.

And I am subjected to Christ as well. I have put myself under His authority, and I am loved. So, death, who is not loved by the Lord of Life, is denied power also over me. Even me!

And Jesus will do this for you if you believe!

"Truly, truly, I say to you, they who hear My word and believe Him who sent Me, have eternal life; they do not come into judgment, but have passed from death to life!" (John 5:24).

"I am the resurrection and the life; they who believe in me, though they die, yet shall they live; and whoever lives and believes in me shall never die!" (John 11:25–26).

This is Easter!

More Than Conquerors

What then are we to say about these things?
If God is for us, who is against us?
He who did not withhold his own Son,
but gave him up for all of us,
will he not with him also give us everything else?
Who will bring any charge against God's elect?
It is God who justifies. Who is to condemn?
It is Christ Jesus, who died, yes, who was raised,
who is at the right hand of God, who indeed intercedes for us.
Who will separate us from the love of Christ?
Will hardship, or distress, or persecution,
or famine, or nakedness, or peril, or sword?
As it is written,
"For your sake we are being killed all day long;
we are accounted as sheep to be slaughtered."
No, in all these things
we are more than conquerors
through him who loved us.
For I am convinced that neither death, nor life, nor angels,
nor rulers, nor things present, nor things to come,
nor powers, nor height, nor depth,
nor anything else in all creation,
will be able to separate us
from the love of God in Christ Jesus our Lord.

—ROMANS 8:31–39

"*We are more than conquerors!*" (8:37) Not only do we—we who believe in and follow Jesus, who accept Him as Lord, who trust in His grace, and who hope in His glory—not only do we conquer, overcome, rise above the difficulties, the persecutions, the tribulations and trials of this worldly life—we are *more* than conquerors! Even though we may be considered as sheep to be slaughtered, we know that, because God loves us, we are "victors in the midst of strife!"

What can I say? Paul says: "What shall we say?" (v. 31). We, who believe, who love the Lord, who are called according to His purpose—His purpose of Life, of Grace, of Salvation—we who are being conformed to the likeness of God's Son, who are justified, who are glorified in Christ Jesus—what shall *we* say? We say that "if God is for us, who can be against us!" (8:31b). Our confidence is not in this world but in Jesus Christ! Our optimism is in knowing, trusting, relying on the fact that God is for us!

With the Big Guy on our side, no bully can threaten us. Nothing malicious can get to us. Nothing can corrupt us, as long as we are with Him. No one can bring any charge against us. They may try, but it will not stick. God, our faith in God, will justify us. No one can condemn us because we follow the One who was condemned for us. But more than that, after He was condemned and whipped and nailed and bled and suffered and died … and was buried … He was *raised to life!*" And He now *"sits at the right hand of God!"* Even more than that, He is also interceding for us," (34), praying for us, sustaining us by the invisible power of His grace at work within and around us, protecting us, continuing to change us, drawing us like a magnet to the truth.

"He who did not spare His own Son, but gave Him up for us all, how will He not also, along with His Son, graciously give us all things?" (v. 32). God's grace is abundant—all things—we have received "grace upon grace"—prevenient grace to prick our conscience; convincing grace to awaken us to our fallen, sinful state and lead us to repentance; justifying grace to set us right with Jesus; and sanctifying grace to sustain us and spur us on in the journey of our faith. John Wesley said that we sin not because we do not have grace, but because we do not use the grace we have! And before we can take hold of that grace we must be as surrendered as our Lord was, from Gethsemane through Golgotha, crying out, "Not my will, but Yours be done!" (Matthew 26:39). And in that surrender is a perfect trust in the love of God, the active, perfect, redeeming love of God that in Christ takes away the sin of the world!

And though it might seem contrary to have to surrender to become conquerors, we learn that we are more than conquerors, despite "persecution, or famine, or nakedness, or danger, or sword, we are more than conquerors through Him who loved us!" (36–37). The grace of God convinces us that "Neither death nor life, neither angels nor demons, neither the present nor the future, nor any powers, neither height nor depth, nor anything else in all creation will be able to separate us from the love of God that is in Christ Jesus our Lord!" (38–39). Nothing from without can separate us from Christ Jesus!

But … ohhh … we can separate ourselves. We can doubt, we can choose not to trust, not to be surrendered, not to accept God's love in Jesus. We can imagine that God is not really *for* us, that the world is *against* us, that we have not been blessed and chosen by adoption to be God's sons and daughters, heirs of God and coheirs with Christ Jesus. We can separate ourselves, believing we need only a strong self-reliance and an independent resolve to rise above the tribulations of this world, to find the path to eternal life and the Way to the kingdom of heaven. Soon enough, though, we learn that we are wrong.

Sometimes, our self-will, our arrogance, our pride can leave us imagining that we can make it on our own, that we can even will ourselves into heaven. Forget about whether there will be a moment of judgment; we want to justify ourselves rather than God. Sometimes we disregard God's truth in scripture because it might say something we just don't like, or we imagine it is only a collection of cute stories that are more fable than fact, more myth than history. But—and here is a great big but—would you disregard the reality of the existence of Jesus? That He died on a cross? That He was buried in a tomb?

Well, now, if He didn't rise from the dead, if He wasn't resurrected, where, then, where is the body? Surely over the years His body would have been found! But, you see, the resurrection is the proof that His suffering and death were for us. He died for us, the innocent for the guilty, the righteous for the unrighteous. And He did so out of love for us. And that love is always there whether we accept it or not. Nothing can separate us from the love of God in Christ Jesus our Lord! But, for it to connect, we need to accept it. And then, when we accept it, a glorious feeling comes over us, an assurance, and it's like suddenly being on top of the world— more than conquerors!

Triumph with Philippians 2:1–11:

If there is any encouragement in Christ,
any consolation from love,
any sharing in the Spirit,
any compassion and sympathy,
make my joy complete:
be of the same mind, having the same love,
being in full accord and of one mind.
Do nothing from selfish ambition or conceit,
but in humility regard others as better than yourselves.
Let each of you look not to your own interests,
but to the interests of others.
Let the same mind be in you that was in Christ Jesus,
who, though he was in the form of God,
did not regard equality with God as something to be exploited,
but emptied himself, taking the form of a slave,
being born in human likeness.
And being found in human form,
he humbled himself and became obedient to the point of death—
even death on a cross.
Therefore God also highly exalted him
and gave him the name that is above every name,
so that at the name of Jesus every knee should bend,
in heaven and on earth and under the earth,
and every tongue should confess that Jesus Christ is Lord,
to the glory of the Father.

The Tomb and the Triumph

Now there was a good and righteous man named Joseph,
who, though a member of the council,
had not agreed to their plan and action.
He came from the Jewish town of Arimathea,
and was waiting expectantly for the kingdom of God.
This man went to Pilate and asked for the body of Jesus.
Then he took it down, wrapped it in a linen cloth,
and laid it in a rock-hewn tomb where no one had ever been laid.
It was the day of Preparation, and the sabbath was beginning.
The women who had come with him from Galilee followed,
and they saw the tomb and how his body was laid.
Then they returned, and prepared spices and ointments.
On the sabbath they rested according to the commandment.
But on the first day of the week,
at early dawn,
they came to the tomb, taking the spices that they had prepared.
They found the stone rolled away from the tomb,
but when they went in, they did not find the body.

—LUKE 23:50–24:3

THE TOMB

The place in which our Lord was laid to rest became the place from which our Lord was raised eternal!

The tomb. A grave. Death. An end. A dead end. Originally, what would have been expected there was decay, deterioration, rottenness, hopelessness. But what it became because of Christ is just the opposite. It is a place of life—life eternal!

The tomb. An actual place. Carved by hard and long labor in the granite of an actual ancient hillside. Not a vault above ground, built with blocks of stone that could have been dismantled and, in time, no trace of its existence could be seen. Not a chamber among other chambers in a catacomb that was hidden underneath the earth, whose access was secret. Not a grave, a hole in the ground, above which a monument, trying to be permanent, but only temporary, might be placed in memorial. Jesus was laid in a tomb. It could not be moved. It was permanent. It was in plain view. Supposedly, it can still be seen today. It could be looked upon as the location where the dead body of Jesus was graciously laid, not by his close friends or family, but by a kind official. It is looked upon as the place from which Jesus was raised!

The tomb. Not borrowed but donated. Never used before, nor after. A temporary place for God incarnate, God-with-us, God almighty. Though dead, Jesus would rise to new life. Not old life, not the way He used to be, but to a newness never known before. The Body of Jesus was eternal. It was the greatest miracle of all.

And it has changed everything. It changed the way His disciples were thinking. It proved to them without a doubt that Jesus was *the* Christ, the true Son of God, the savior of the world. It proved that One without sin became the sacrifice for all sin. It proved that the love of God for you and me was willing to take our place as a ransom for our souls. It proved that the power of God is greater than death.

Did you need proof? Consider the tomb. Consider the stone that guarded its entrance. Consider its unexpected emptiness. Let the unbelievable make you a believer because it is believable! When you begin to see through the lens of the resurrection, it all becomes believable. Later, apostle Paul would write:

> If Christ has not been raised, then our proclamation has been in vain and your faith has been in vain. We are even found to be misrepresenting God ... because we testified of God that He raised Christ (whom God did not raise if it is true that the dead are not raised). For if the dead are not raised, then Christ has not been raised. If Christ has not been raised, your faith is futile, and you are still in your sins. Then those who have fallen asleep in Christ have perished.

If for this life only we have hoped in Christ, we are of
all people the most to be pitied." (1 Corinthians 15:14–19)

The entire existence of the church is based on the promise of the reality
of the resurrection. If the resurrection is not true, then we have all been
fooled because the resurrection proves to us that Jesus is the Son of God.
If He has not been raised, He cannot be the Son of God. And if He is not
the Son of God, we are fools for believing in Him. But "When they went
in (to the tomb), they did not find the Body!"

They weren't at the wrong tomb. "They saw the tomb and how His
Body was laid" (v. 55b). "The women who had come with Jesus from
Galilee" (55a) were not just curious. They were purposeful. They went
away, perhaps finding the home of the one who had provided the Upper
Room for Christ's Passover with His disciples. It is not really known exactly
where they might have gone. It might even have been to the home of Mary
and Martha in Bethany. These women were from Galilee; they didn't
have a place to stay in Jerusalem. But they went "and prepared spices and
ointments" … to anoint Jesus's body … later.

But that was at the end of the day, Friday. The next day, which began
at sunset on Friday, was the Sabbath. The day of rest. They could not go
to the tomb that day. No work could be done; only so many steps could be
taken. On such an important feast—which lasted seven days—the Feast
of Unleavened Bread—which began with the Passover—they knew they
should not defy the Sabbath ordinances. Not in Jerusalem.

So, they waited. Meanwhile, the body of Jesus lay in the tomb.

It was the tomb of Joseph of Arimathea. He was a member of the
Sanhedrin—the council of elders, the leaders of Judaism. Luke tells us
that Joseph "had not agreed to their plan of action" when they sought
to arrest Jesus, try Him, and have Him executed. Joseph of Arimathea,
Luke tells, "was waiting expectantly for the Kingdom of God." Did
that simply mean he was old and was looking forward to dying? Did
it mean he believed the coming of the kingdom was imminent? Did it
mean he thought Jesus had had the power to conjure an army to defeat
the Romans and return Israel to the Jews? John, in the fourth Gospel,
gives us the only other clue. There, it says of Joseph of Arimathea that
he was "a disciple of Jesus, though secretly …, for fear of the Jews" (John

19:38). And in John he has a partner in the burial of Jesus—Nicodemus (39–40).

Some scholars see Joseph of Arimathea as a bit of a tragic figure. There is no word that he raised his voice against the actions of the council. And though I can believe he did, he was probably well outnumbered and hushed when he tried. But maybe he did keep silent out of fear. Maybe he kept his distance from the council, knowing he was powerless to stop their course of action. Whatever his posture, whatever his thoughts, his heart was moved to offer to the Lord the last blessing the earthly Jesus would receive. The women thought the same. In fact, theirs would have been the very last blessing, but the anointing of His body would never be done.

But one of the tragedies of this life is that the honor we offer when someone has died could well have been given when they were alive. Often, we are haunted by the things we wished we'd done, or the words we wished we'd spoken before a loved one died. And out of a painful sense of our own lack, we offer a blessing that those who have died may never really know. But, we know it, and so we do it. And Joseph of Arimathea is remembered as the one who offered his own tomb so that the body of Christ would not be left to the dogs and the birds of prey.

And that tomb would become a reminder to us, almost two thousand years later, that Joseph of Arimathea was a believer, a generous man, a man who wanted to offer some honorable and tangible legacy in the name of his Lord. And so should we! Not a tomb, necessarily, but a blessing.

And because, later, that tomb was empty, and the Lord had risen, it was no longer an object of tragedy, or hopelessness, of decay and despair. That tomb became a sign of triumph!

THE TRIUMPH

Luke says nothing about any soldiers guarding the tomb. They are only mentioned in the Gospel of Matthew. In Matthew, at the moment the stone was rolled away, there was an earthquake. And the angel who moved the stone looked like lightning. "And the guards shook in fear, and became like dead men" (Matthew 28:4). That moment of fear is known by the women in Luke, but it is because two angels were suddenly standing beside them. At first, they were just perplexed. But the fog of their confusion is quickly sliced through with a terror that blinded them, and they bowed their faces to the earth. The divine presence was far too much for them to bear.

Unseen, at that very moment, I imagine a glorious cheer of victory in the heavenly realm. The host of heaven was chanting: "Death is swallowed up in victory!" "O Death, where is thy sting!" "O Hades, where is thy victory!" (1 Corinthians 15:54–55).

Before the triumph of Christ was known, or had even begun to be understood on earth, there would have been great rejoicing in heaven. Dawn was breaking. The heavens were silent, waiting. Two angels, sent to earth to open the tomb, arrive on the scene. One steps over to the stone. He begins to position himself, hands in place, feet finding their stance. He bends, and leans in with his shoulder, and … push! How long would an angel have had to strain to move a stone like that? It moves. It rolls. It is out of the way. The angel had triumphed. The whole earth shook with the victory!

The tomb was open. Unseen by human eyes, unknown by human understanding, the next moment saw Christ rise! The glorious praise for the triumph of the angel was magnified a thousand times when Christ arose! How it happened, what took place in that moment, is unknown. But it happened. It must have been glorious!

But for mortal minds, unable to see or comprehend what God was doing on Easter morning, there was only confusion. The heavenly host, observing it all, may have moved to the edge of their seats, hoping, waiting, longing to see the triumph of belief. Slowly. … slowly, the women absorb it all. Their faces were still bowed to the ground, but their ears were open. "Why do you look for the living among the dead?" For the moment, the question makes absolutely no sense. They had seen Jesus's body laid to rest inside that tomb. They were not looking for someone who was living; they were looking for someone who was dead!

"He is not here! He has risen!" What does that mean? By the time of Christ, there was an understanding that a resurrection of some kind would occur on the last day, but it would be universal. Daniel spoke of it (Daniel 12:1–4). It would be wonderful. It would be glorious. Had that moment come? Were they experiencing the fulfillment of all time? The angelic host is tense, hoping, waiting. The women were confused. "Remember how

He told you, while He was still in Galilee, that the Son of Man must be handed over to sinners, and be crucified, and on the third day rise again?!" And they remembered! Triumph!

No. Wait! They still don't get it. Luke simply says that they returned from the tomb, their jars of spice unopened, and they found the eleven, and "all the rest" (whoever they are), and told them that two angels said that Jesus had risen! Did *they* believe? How did they tell them? Were they worried because the body was gone? The tomb was empty! That certainly meant something! But what?

Their words seemed only like an idle tale. They did not believe the women. Even though they could back each other up, and that was supposed to be proof enough in a court of law, they just couldn't accept it. But the heavenly host knew it was true! They would have wanted to intervene, touch their minds in some way to make them realize that the most glorious miracle of all time had just happened. Maybe something did touch one of them.

Suddenly, Peter got up and ran out. He raced to the tomb. Yes! The stone had been rolled away! He braced himself, moved slowly down to the opening. He stooped down and looked in. Yes! He saw that the body was gone, just the linen cloths were left. Did he get it? Luke says only, "then he went home." But he adds that "he was amazed at what had happened." He just wasn't *there* yet.

And all the heavenly host sigh and sit back into their seats, knowing, understanding, waiting, eager to watch the next scene where the triumph of belief would finally come to those who were mortal. But they were satisfied, pleased, with the amazement that filled Peter's heart. Where is that amazement today?

They wait, watching and hoping, eager to see the triumph come to every heart.

And that is the posture of the heavenly host as they observe us. Some of us are like the women, confused by it all. Some of us are like Peter, stunned with amazement. Could it be that, unseen, watching over us, over each one of us, is a host of angels, knowing that the triumph of the resurrection, the resurrection power is moving in each of our lives, stirring in us not just a new belief but a deeper belief, not just an acceptance of the truth but an understanding of it all; not just a sense of amazement but of great joy. And they're hoping to see a triumph, a great and wonderful triumph, and they will rejoice gloriously when we are born again, when we choose faith as we are tempted, when we show love when we are hurt, when we seek peace in our distress, when we rise above our fears, when we rise above our worries, when we look up when we are low, and when we seek light amid darkness and life amid death.

The triumph has come, and it is waiting. It is waiting for us to embrace it, to sing the resurrection song, to proclaim with all our hearts what Josh Groban wrote in his song, sung by the group Selah: (Find it, please. Let it inspire you!)

"You Raise Me Up"
When I am down, and oh my soul, so weary;
When troubles come, and my heart burdened be.
Then I am still and wait here in the silence,
Until You come and sit awhile with me.
You raise me up so I can stand on mountains.
You raise me up to walk on stormy seas.
I am strong when I am on Your shoulders.
You raise me up to more than I can be.
There is no life, no life without its hunger.
Each restless heart beats so imperfectly.
But when you come, and I am filled with wonder.
Sometimes I think I glimpse eternity.
You raise me up.

PART 2
The Resurrection in Matthew

The stories of the resurrection in Matthew have a special attraction for me. I'm not sure exactly why, but I love to picture the angel sitting on the great stone beside the tomb after rolling it away from the opening. It tickles my funny bone. It's like, "Take *that*, Satan! Ha-ha!" I am challenged by the efforts of the chief priests and Pharisees to control things both by setting a guard and by trying to cover things up by bribing them later. But it is only in Matthew that there are guards, and they faint dead away when the resurrection happens. I imagine the women almost stepping over them carefully as they approach the tomb a few moments later. I picture them as they are careful not to awaken them, while, at the same time, they wonder what could have happened to them. The contrast between the guards and the women is remarkable. It is almost comedic! Maybe it is supposed to be funny. Still, the resurrection becomes a very joyful moment, inspiring us all to just love the story. Please, love it with me.

"Truly, this man was the son of God"

Now when the centurion and those with him,
who were keeping watch over Jesus,
saw the earthquake and what took place,
they were terrified and said,
"Truly this man was God's Son!"

—MATTHEW 27:54

What goes through your mind as you consider how the one Roman centurion stood facing the cross, watching Christ die. Have you ever watched someone die? A moment comes that's very much like the feeling you get when a cloud moves in to block the sun. For some, it's the sense that *something* just happened; something happened that made you look. For others, it's a combined sense of a very strong presence and a very desolate absence. For still others, it's a mixture of joy and loss. Somehow, though, the sudden emptiness is not just a bare nonexistence. It is as much an arrival as it is a departure. But something is different. Different because a change occurs.

The centurion stood by for about six hours, watching Jesus die. The clouds moved in to block the sun and "there was darkness over the whole land" from the sixth hour until the ninth hour, from noon until three o'clock. And the centurion watched. He had listened to Christ's tormentors; he had heard Jesus cry out in forsakenness, and he saw Jesus cry out and breathe his last. But when he saw Jesus die, he saw more than just one man's death. He saw my death and he saw your death too. For Jesus Christ died for us! And I believe that the centurion saw that Jesus died for him too, and the gratitude and grace that right then filled his heart brought such an overwhelming recognition of the grace of God that he was inspired enough to proclaim that "truly, this man was the Son of God."

Jesus didn't just die for what he believed. And he didn't just die as a sacrifice for sin. Christ's death changed death forever. Because of what God did in Jesus Christ, death can no longer be considered as just the end of life, but as a change. "Lo! I tell you a mystery, We shall not all sleep, but we shall all be changed … For this perishable nature must put on the imperishable" (1 Corinthians 15; 51, 53).

And because death is different, our lives can be different. We no longer need to live as though this was all there is. In fact, there is something so far greater than "this" that we should not only live for it as a future possibility for us at the end of our earthly life but as something that is happening even now. Jesus Christ himself proclaimed the kingdom of heaven as a reality that was at hand way back in the first century. And yet believers still seem to live their lives as though they must do so much, accumulate so many experiences, gain so many things before they die; while, in the meantime, they know that real life comes when we are changed. None of those things really matters, except one: The experience that Jesus Christ is the son of God.

The centurion had an experience so vivid and so inspiring that he was able to say, "Truly, this man was the Son of God!" But the truth of the matter was, and still is, that Jesus Christ *is* the Son of God. As much as Christ's death altered death for us, Christ's rising from death brings a whole new meaning to our lives. We stand, as did the centurion on Calvary, facing the cross, bearing witness to the change that Jesus Christ is making in our lives. For by His death, we are changed from sinners into servants. And His rising from death has changed the fallen state of human nature.

It may be a comforting thing to believe in the empty tomb, but many who do are disturbed by the bloody cross. We can't have one without the other.

We must be changed. It's a reassuring thing to follow the Son of God who takes away the sin of the world, but many fall short of the calling of the son of man who came to seek and to save the lost. We can't have one without the other. We must be changed. It's a glorious thing to be born anew by the Spirit. But many who claim it are not moved to the point of sacrifice. We can't have one without the other. We must be changed. It's a joy to have hope in our rising with Christ. But all too few will identify with Him in His death. We can't have one without the other. We must be changed.

Whatever it was that compelled the centurion as he faced the cross when Jesus died, it is still compelling people today. It may have happened nearly two thousand years ago, but it changed my life!

It can change your life too if you let yourself be changed.

Dead and Buried

Many women were also there, looking on from a distance;
they had followed Jesus from Galilee and had provided for him.
Among them were Mary Magdalene, and Mary the mother of James and Joseph,
and the mother of the sons of Zebedee.
When it was evening,
there came a man from Arimathea, named Joseph,
who was also a disciple of Jesus.
He went to Pilate and asked for the body of Jesus;
then Pilate ordered it to be given to him.
So Joseph took the body and wrapped it in a clean linen cloth,
and laid it in his own new tomb, which he had hewn from the rock.
He rolled a great stone to the door of the tomb and went away.
Mary Magdalene and the other Mary were there, sitting opposite the tomb.
The next day,
that is, after the day of Preparation,
the chief priests and the Pharisees gathered before Pilate
and said, "Sir, we remember what that imposter said while he was still alive,
'After three days I will rise again.'
Therefore command the tomb to be made secure until the third day,
otherwise his disciples may go and steal him away,
and tell the people, 'He has been raised from the dead,'
and the last deception would be worse than the first."
Pilate told them,
"You have a guard of soldiers; go make it as secure as you can."
So they went with the guard and made the tomb secure by
sealing the stone.

—MATTHEW 27:55–66

End of story!? Not!
We know it's not over. *We* know the rest of the story. We're even part of it! We are believers. Christians. Jesus was dead and buried. They thought it was over. They did everything they could to put a period

at the end of the sentence. Buried. "They went with the guard and made the tomb secure by sealing the stone" (v. 66).

But we know. Not just because there's still another chapter in the Gospel of Matthew, but because Jesus rose. If He didn't, we've all been fooled. Paul said: "If for this life only we have hoped in Christ, we are of all people most to be pitied!" (1 Corinthians 15:19).

The world wants to leave Jesus in the tomb. We, who believe, have heard the angel say it over and over: "He is not here. He has been raised!" (28:6). But for those who can't believe it, or won't believe it because they are too practical—so practical in fact that they scoff at the idea of miracles, at the notion of mystery, at the amazement of wonder—they won't let go of what they see as flaws in the story, or inconsistencies between the Gospels. Some might be unwilling to accept intellectually anything that suggests that the spiritual is real, or that the soul exists, let alone is eternal. They think they're too intelligent to fall for this stuff. It is not intelligence; it is a lack of trust, a lack of faith.

So why did they need a guard? Because they thought, "His disciples may go and steal him away, and tell the people, 'He has been raised from the dead' and the last deception would be worse than the first" (27:64). How arrogant! How insecure! And yet how practical. They thought they could be smarter than God!

> The message about the Cross is foolishness to those who are perishing, but to us who are being saved it is the power of God For it is written, "I will destroy the wisdom of the wise, and the discernment of the discerning I will thwart." Where is the one who is wise? Where is the scribe? Where is the debater of this age? Has not God made foolish the wisdom of the world? For since, in the wisdom of God, the world did not know God though wisdom, God decided, through the foolishness of our proclamation, to save those who believe. For Jews demand signs and Greeks desire wisdom, but we proclaim Christ crucified—a stumbling block to the Jews and foolishness to the Gentiles, but to those who are called, both Jews and Greeks, Christ—the power of God and the wisdom of

God. For God's foolishness is wiser than human wisdom, and God's weakness is stronger than human strength. (1 Corinthians 1:18–25)

With sarcastic wit, Paul uses the notion of foolishness to refute human logic. And though Paul is talking about the message of the cross, the message of the resurrection was probably even more foolish in the minds of those who couldn't fathom the reality of someone rising from the dead. Logic cannot interpret human experience, let alone begin to understand divine purposes. That's where the chief priests and the Pharisees were stuck. Foolishness!?

"Many women were there" (Matthew 27:55). They had watched Jesus die. They had heard the words spoken by the centurion at the moment of His Death: "Truly this man was the Son of God!" (27:54). Some of them are named by Matthew. After the Sabbath, (according to Matthew) two of the Marys would go to the tomb. Perhaps they had already begun discussing how they might honor Jesus when the time was right.

Meanwhile, another practical man—Joseph of Arimathea—thought clearly enough to do the functional work of taking Jesus's body and laying it in his own newly excavated tomb. The two Marys saw it all. Joseph was practical in that he did what was needed while others were only wringing their hands or cowering in fear. But Joseph, though one of *them*—a member of the council of Elders—was a disciple. He saw in Jesus a truth the doubters could not see. And what he did honored Jesus!

It's not over when it's over. Love doesn't end when someone dies. Even doubters know this. Even nonbelievers. There's something wonderful within that continues to reach out in their direction. It's something mysterious that can't make clear sense in this lifetime. And when we don't fully understand something, we often make up our own explanations. The chief priests and the Pharisees explained away the resurrection by propagating the story that the disciples had stolen Jesus's body from the tomb—the last deception—and were then lying to everyone that He had risen from death.

But we, who believe, trust the story. Our faith could not possibly be based on a lie. Jesus died for our sins, but He rose to bring us the assurance of life eternal. There comes a point when to doubt is to rebel, where to be unwilling to accept the grace of God in Christ is to deny its possibilities; it is to reject the truth. I believe that when it's over, when we have finished our course in this world and come before the gates of heaven, we will discover that all doubt was really self-doubt. We doubted because we were just not yet able to understand, and because there were things we couldn't understand, we couldn't accept the truths that others proclaimed. Paul, himself, confessed: "For now we see in a mirror dimly, but then we will see face to face. Now I know only in part, then I shall understand fully" (1 Corinthians 13:12). Patience … and we'll understand it better bye and bye.

For now, we know there was a time when Jesus was dead and buried, grave-guarded, stone-sealed, end of story. And it was and is a reason to grieve. For doubters maybe it was a reason to gloat. But that was almost two thousand years ago! Something amazing must have happened for the story to last this long!

Christ is risen! He is risen indeed!

I Know You Are Looking for Jesus

After the sabbath, as the first day of the week was dawning,
Mary Magdalene and the other Mary went to see the tomb.
And suddenly there was a great earthquake;
for an angel of the Lord, descending from heaven,
came and rolled back the stone
and sat on it.
His appearance was like lightning, and his clothing white as snow.
For fear of him the guards shook and became like dead men.
But the angel said to the women,
"Do not be afraid,
I know that you are looking for Jesus who was crucified.
He is not here
for he has been raised,
as he said.
Come, see the place where he lay.
Then go quickly and tell his disciples,
'He has been raised from the dead and indeed he is going ahead of you
to Galilee, there you will see him.'
This is my message to you."

—MATTHEW 28:1–7

The ground suddenly shook violently beneath their feet. They reeled and fell down, holding on to themselves, or to each other for what seemed like far too long. They were on their way to the grave of their wonderful teacher, intending to wash the blood off His body and anoint it with fragrant oils and myrrh. It was a small and bittersweet task. The sun was rising.

The Sabbath was over, and they could work again, they could take more steps now. They could go to the tomb of Jesus. But for this moment—this incredibly long moment—they wondered if they were going to make it. Everything was shaking. At that exact same time, beyond their line of sight, something so earth-shaking, so mind-shattering, so drastically life-altering was happening that the world has never been the same since. An angel had come, appearing from out of nowhere, or everywhere, like lightning; he moved to the great stone that had been set in front of the tomb, and, with herculean strength, rolled it away from the opening. It was a rare and glorious task. The Son was rising! The Son of God.

With a combination of joy and exhaustion, the angel then sat down on that stone, triumphant over the obstacle at the tomb, just moments before the women would arrive. It must have been quite strange for them, as they approached the burial site of their teacher, to see the Roman guards lying, out like stones, on the ground nearby. The earthquake? Maybe. The angel? Yes!

But then, before they even saw the angel, he spoke to them telling them not to be afraid. I imagine a gasp. They were suddenly breathless, speechless. And the angel said, "I know you are looking for Jesus!"

Yes! They *were* looking for Jesus. They wanted to see Him one more time. They wanted to honor Him by anointing His body. They wanted to cry through their grief as they fulfilled this one last mournful duty for Him. It was their way of saying goodbye.

To the world, the church is the angel sitting on the stone. To whoever comes, we need to say, "I know you are looking for Jesus." For everyone who walks through our doors, something earth-shaking and life-altering has either happened, or will happen, or is happening now, and whether they are seriously seeking, or they're not really sure of what they're expecting to find, we know they are looking for Jesus. Will they find Him here?

We are stationed at the empty tomb. We know we follow, we serve, a risen savior. We know who Jesus is. We know He is God-incarnate. We know His death means our redemption. And we know His resurrection is the proof that Jesus is the Christ. And, like the angel, "we know you are looking for Jesus!"

"He is not here!" Not the way you think He should be. Not the way the world imagines. Not a dead teacher, not a martyred healer, not a rebellious liberator; not just the subject of our devotion, and not just a memory.

"He is risen!" Jesus is a living presence in our lives. Yes, the real body of our crucified and buried Lord was raised. That body, wounds and all, walked alive, moved among the disciples for forty days. But then He ascended. "I know you are looking for Jesus."

What you will find, now, are people who love Him; people who know who He is, and He is a part of our lives. He is a part of who I am. He is a part of who we are. Our lives have been altered and are still being altered.

Now, whenever we gather in His name, even if it's just two or three of us, He is present (Matthew 18:20). Christ is King. He reigns in our lives, in our church, in our hearts. He is present because His kingdom is present. He said, "The Kingdom of God is not coming with signs that can be observed; nor will they say, 'Look, here it is!' or 'There it is!' For, in fact, the Kingdom of God is among you!" (Luke 17:20–21).

Sitting on the Stone

After the sabbath, as the first day of the week was dawning,
Mary Magdalene and the other Mary went to see the tomb.
And suddenly there was a great earthquake;
for an angel of the Lord, descending from heaven,
came and rolled back the stone
and sat on it.
His appearance was like lightning, and his clothing white as snow.
For fear of him the guards shook and became like dead men.
But the angel said to the women,
"Do not be afraid,
I know that you are looking for Jesus who was crucified.
He is not here;
for he has been raised,
as he said.
Come, see the place where he lay.
Then go quickly and tell his disciples,
'He has been raised from the dead and indeed he is going ahead of you
to Galilee, there you will see him'
This is my message to you.
So they left the tomb quickly with fear and great joy,
and ran to tell his disciples.
Suddenly Jesus met them and said,
"Greetings!"
And they came to him, took hold of his feet, and worshiped him.
Then Jesus said to them, "Do not be afraid;
go and tell my brothers to go to Galilee; there they will see me."
While they were going,
some of the guard went into the city
and told the chief priests everything that had happened.

—MATTHEW 28:1–11

I t was still dark. Maybe the sky was just beginning to brighten, but it was still dark. Two women named Mary have come to the grave of their healer, their forgiver, their savior, their friend. They are grieving.

They are lost in sorrow. Perhaps, they are even angry at the way such a good man had to suffer and die. But they came to the place where their Lord had been laid. Matthew's story makes no reference to their intentions, he states no reason for their coming other than to see the sepulcher (v. 1). We might assume that they had hopes of anointing Jesus and covering his graveclothes with spices, because this is their reason for coming to the tomb in the Gospels of Mark and Luke. But they came, and it couldn't be easy. Going to the grave of a loved one is difficult at first, because of the loss. It takes some time before going to the grave brings a sense of peace or of thanksgiving that the one that was so loved is at rest.

The moment of their arrival throws them into confusion, though, because "there was a great earthquake" (v. 2). Even if it only lasted for a few seconds, it must have been terrifying. Already, at the moment of Jesus's death a few days before, according to Matthew, there was an earthquake so severe that "the rocks were split" and the dead were wakened! (27:51–53). I imagine that the terrible rumbling they now suddenly felt brought back the same excruciating pangs of that dreadful moment when they saw and heard Jesus cry out with a loud voice as He yielded up His Spirit and died (27:50). The whole world seems out of control as it shakes in an earthquake. You can't tell what will happen next. All of existence seems to be shattering, falling apart. It must have been very unsettling, let alone frightening.

How has your world been shaken lately? What spiritual earthquakes have you undergone? How did you recover? Who helped you steady yourself?

It was an angel! The very presence of the power of God! "His appearance was like lightning; and his raiment white as snow" (v. 3). Awesome! Amazing! Terrifying! The angel rolled back the stone from in front of the tomb to show the women that Jesus was not there. And nearby these big Roman centurions guarding the tomb, toughened by battle, hardened by war, these brave and fearless men of valor with backbones of steel and the courage of lions, they tremble with fear, and they faint dead away.

But look at the angel! After he rolled back the stone, what did he do? He "sat on it!" His posture becomes one of rest, one of ease. He does not take a stance of defiance! He is not necessarily intimidating. He looks friendly, hospitable, inviting. But still … awesome! This sudden calm after the violent earthquake brings such a relief, such a peace, that it almost feels like a breath of fresh air. The resurrection!

It evokes great wonder! "Do not be afraid," (v. 5) the angel said to the women. "I know you are looking for Jesus who was crucified, but He's not here. He has risen, just as he said He would! Come closer. Look into the tomb. This is where He used to lay."

This is the most incredible moment of all time since God finished His act of creation, and God's angel seems almost casual! There was just an earthquake! And the angel seems almost nonchalant! But, you see, the angel knew. The angel knew what was going on. The angel knew that, though this was an awesome occasion, there was no cause for fear. He rolled away the stone from in front of the tomb and almost playfully hiked himself up and sat on top of it. The earthquake ends, the guards pass out, and the two women named Mary, probably stunned half to death, look up, and there he is, sitting on the stone! And he's saying, "Don't be afraid!"

How can you be afraid of an angel who has just plopped himself down on the top of a big stone? His posture is not fearful. It is not challenging, but invitational, welcoming. And this is the gift of the resurrection! "Come. See." Witness for yourself the wonderful power of God. "Then … go quickly … go quickly and tell his disciples he has risen from the dead!" (v. 6). Don't keep it to yourself, bear witness to the good news. And do so with a sense of urgency! Echoes of the last words of Christ in the Gospel of Matthew: "Go … and tell … Go, make disciples. Baptize them … and tell them all that I have told you!"

So, they departed quickly from the tomb with fear … and … great joy! (v. 8). Filled with new feelings, and some old fears, and perhaps even some new fears, they hurry to tell the other disciples. Matthew says they ran! So, they're running along in the early light of a new day, when all of a sudden, they receive another shock that stops them in their tracks! You can almost see them nearly running past Him, or nearly running into Him. But Jesus meets them on their way. Did they practically trip Him in their excitement when they came up to Him and took hold of His feet and worshiped Him? How do you picture the scene?

How great it would be to see alive the very one you had watched die! How thankful they must have been. How amazed they must have felt as the reality sank in that the power of the resurrection was so real. How deep their honor! How glorious their praise! How thunderous their fears!

"Then Jesus said to them, 'Do not be afraid …'"' (v. 10).

Catch your breath now. Settle down. Yes, it is awesome! Yes, it is amazing! This is the power of the resurrection. Can you feel it? Can you feel it working in your life? Aren't you amazed? Isn't it magnificent? This is the power of faith that tells us, with Paul, that "if while we were enemies we were reconciled to God by the death of His Son, much more, now that we are reconciled, shall we be saved by His life!" (Romans 5:10).

How glorious! What an amazing grace it is that we have received! What a wonderful love we have all been given! What a beautiful gift it is that we are able to share! Do not be afraid.

Do not be afraid!

Risen and Alive

Suddenly,
Jesus met them and said,
"Greetings!"
And they came to him, took hold of his feet,
and worshiped him.
Then Jesus said to them,
"Do not be afraid;
go and tell my brothers to go to Galilee; there they will see me."

—MATTHEW 28:9–10

Guards had been posted. The stone before the opening of the tomb had been sealed. Jesus was dead and buried. No one was going to steal His body. No one. Period.

Suddenly … suddenly … suddenly … "there was a great earthquake" (28:2). Just as the sun began to rise, just as it was beginning to be bright enough to see clearly, "an angel of the Lord, descending from heaven, came and rolled back the stone … and sat on it! His appearance was like lightning, and his clothing white as snow!" (vv. 2b–3).

The two Marys saw it. The guards saw it too. It terrified them so much that, for a while, they became catatonic! Unable to respond. Unable to move. Unable to think. They fell to the ground. It doesn't say much for them, hardened soldiers that they were, that they fainted. But in their defense, it was something supernatural that was happening. It might be enough to endure the terror of an earthquake, and this was "a *great* earthquake!" But then to see the glory of God in the presence of an angel … well, they were completely freaked out!

They probably knew why they were posted at the tomb. The chief priests and the Pharisees had told Pilate, "Sir, we remember what that imposter said while He was still alive, 'After three days I will rise again!' Therefore we command the tomb to be made secure until the third day!"

(27:63–64). The guards would have known this. It would be eerie to keep vigil through the night near any grave, let alone to guard one that held a man who said He'd rise again. And their nerves might have been on edge thinking that His followers might come to break in and steal the body! Any unexpected noise would have made them jump, would have set them off— battle-ready, heart-pounding, adrenalin-pumping, sword-wielding soldiers that they were. They fainted dead away—"became like dead men" (v. 4).

The women lived through the same earthquake and the same experience of the angel's divine brilliance, but they reacted very differently. Perhaps, because the angel was more in tune with them, they were as comforted by his presence as they were in fear and awe. And, of course, the angel did say to them, "Do not be afraid." In Matthew there is no condescending question such as "Why are you looking for the living among the dead?" as in Luke's story (24:5).

Matthew's version is very friendly. This one angel is downright hospitable, welcoming the women to "Come, see the place where He lay." But the angel then tells them to "Go quickly … tell the disciples, 'He has been raised from the dead,' and indeed He is going ahead of you to Galilee; there you will see Him!"

Now, Galilee was all they could think about! They would see Jesus again, Resurrected, alive!? They had to hurry and tell the others. They were feeling both "fear and great joy!" How awesome! How wonderful! How glorious! They began to run. Then …

Suddenly … suddenly … suddenly … Jesus met them, and said, "Greetings!" Instantly they recognized Him (28:9). What a sweet moment! How wonderful! It was pure worship. It reminds us that inasmuch as we are commanded to worship, we are being invited to fall before Jesus, to grab ahold of His feet, to lavish upon Him our love. Yes, commanded to worship—the fourth commandment: Remember the Sabbath to keep it holy. Remember that there is a moment, a slice of time, when God expects us to enter into His holiness. That was what left the guards catatonic— they couldn't bear the presence of holiness.

The moment of Christ's resurrection was so perfectly holy that even the earth rattled. We need to remember that the resurrection is real, and it's real in our lives. The Christian faith can still rattle the world. But only because that moment is still working in the lives of believers. Because

Christ is risen, we can rise. Because Christ is alive, we are alive and going. We may not be going to Galilee to see the risen Lord. We are His Body—risen and alive, proving His Presence, filled with His Spirit, alive with His grace inspired. Hoping to do what Jesus did; hoping to be what Jesus is. "Do not be afraid; go and tell ..." (28:10). I think we've got the do-not-be-afraid part down. We've still got a lot of telling to do though. Go and tell others where they can find Christ. Let them see His Spirit at work in your life. He is risen and alive in you and me! Believe it! Let Him live! Amen.

Afraid, Yet Filled with Joy

After the sabbath, as the first day of the week was dawning,
Mary Magdalene and the other Mary went to see the tomb.
And suddenly there was a great earthquake;
for an angel of the Lord, descending from heaven,
came and rolled back the stone
and sat on it.
His appearance was like lightning, and his clothing white as snow.
For fear of him the guards shook and became like dead men.
But the angel said to the women,
"Do not be afraid,
I know that you are looking for Jesus who was crucified.
He is not here;
for he has been raised,
as he said.
Come, see the place where he lay.
Then go quickly and tell his disciples,
'He has been raised from the dead and indeed he is going ahead of you
to Galilee, there you will see him'
This is my message to you.
So they left the tomb quickly with fear and great joy,
and ran to tell his disciples.
Suddenly,
Jesus met them and said,
"Greetings!"
And they came to him, took hold of his feet,
and worshiped him.
Then Jesus said to them,
"Do not be afraid;
go and tell my brothers to go to Galilee; there they will see me."

—MATTHEW 28:1-10

Is there a condition of being afraid but not scared? The two who went to look at the tomb of Christ had a mind-altering experience. In Matthew, it says they only went to see the tomb (28:1). In Mark and

Luke, we are told that their purpose was to anoint the body of Jesus with spices. In the unexpected suddenness of their encounter with the angel, the rolled-away stone, and the empty tomb, their purpose was changed into that of becoming the bearers of a very particular message: Christ had "risen from the dead and is going ahead of you to Galilee! There you will see Him" (v. 7).

Jesus had died on Friday! But suddenly, He was going to Galilee!? They would see Him there? They would see Him alive? Is that what made them afraid, or was it that they had seen an angel? Whatever it was, they were "afraid, yet filled with joy!" (28:8).

Afraid, frightened, shocked, startled, stunned in their minds. And yet … joyful, glad, delighted, thrilled, inspired in their hearts. Even though they were apprehensive, they were encouraged. Though terrified, they were confident. Though awestruck, they were charged full of enthusiasm.

I think the whole world is somewhere in the spectrum of those feelings. When it comes to Easter, when it comes to the resurrection of Christ, you can't be indifferent. Not unless your heart has been hardened or your mind is numb.

The experience of God's miraculous realities can sometimes be paralyzing. We just can't absorb so great a truth. We can't believe the inconceivable, But then God's grace goes to work, and the facts that intimidated us at first begin to sink in; they reach our hearts, and they compel us to new depths and propel us to new life. Sometimes, the heart can believe what the mind can't conceive. The mind may resist, but the heart will understand!

They felt a sort of dread, and yet they made haste. They hurried, full of both fear and joy. They began to run. They felt eager despite their anxiety. I picture the women glancing at each other after a dozen steps or so, reaching out, grasping each other's hand, and pulling the other along, thinking, *Let's go!*

The sun was up. The landscape was full of daylight. Jerusalem was beginning to really come alive with business as usual, though not the usual business. It was still the season of the Passover Feast. But these women knew something no one else did. It was extremely out of the ordinary. It was extraordinary. Nothing usual about it. They wanted to tell the disciples.

Suddenly, Jesus met them (v. 9).

He stopped them in their tracks by saying, "Greetings!" For them it may have seemed as if another earthquake was happening—an emotional earthquake. There was a very brief pause, a giant moment of recognition, and then they dissolved into ecstasy, falling before Jesus, clasping His feet, worshiping! (v. 9).

Worshiping. Rejoicing. Filled with gladness. Wrapped up in grace. Relishing the seconds. The angel had said, "Do not be afraid, for I know you are looking for Jesus, who was crucified. He is not here!' (5–6). I imagine a pause at that moment, however brief, when the women were crestfallen by the devastating idea: "He is not here" (v. 6). The lump in their throats began to choke them up as tears welled up in their eyes. And then the angel said, "He has risen!" (6b). Their hearts skip a beat when they hear that news!

And now, they are met by Christ. What joy! What rapture! And now, it is Jesus who says, "Do not be afraid" (10). And I believe it is then and there that a peaceful calm came over them. Still eager, still excited, but now … joy. Just joy! Gladness. Hearts warmed by the presence of Jesus, they felt a perfect sort of assurance, It was pure worship.

But … they were told to "Go" (v. 7). We don't get to stay there. As much as we might want it to last forever, we don't get to stay. There is a purpose beyond us when we have been touched. "Tell … tell my brothers …" (v. 10).

Matthew doesn't tell us what happened next with these two women. He doesn't tell us anything more about the angel of the tomb. But we know where the story goes. It's still being told. And it is we who are speaking. It is we who are filled with joy. It is we who are so glad. It is we who are so inspired. What our minds can't conceive, our hearts have believed! Christ is risen! He is risen indeed!

The Passover Plot

While they were going,
some of the guard went into the city and told the chief priests everything that had happened.
After the priests had assembled with the elders,
they devised a plan to give a large sum of money to the soldiers,
telling them, "You must say,
'His disciples came by night and stole him away while we were asleep.'
If this comes to the governor's ears,
we will satisfy him and keep you out of trouble."
So they did as they were directed.
And this story is still told among the Jews to this day.

—MATTHEW 28:11–15

In his book *The Passover Plot*, Hugh J. Schonfield begins with the premise that the resurrection of Jesus just does not make sense. A human being cannot rise from the dead. So, he sees Jesus as a man of great intelligence and wisdom who had a great hope for humankind and for the inauguration of a kingdom of God. He has no notion of the idea of the Incarnation in what he says. Jesus's whole intention was to "fulfill" as many of the key prophecies about the Messiah as he could, to establish himself as the greatest teacher and redeemer of all time. Using plot and cunning, he contrived a plan that would give obvious impressions of the possibility of his "messiaship." And Jesus was even willing to go so far as to suffer and risk his own death to prove himself invincible.

Associating himself with simple people, and with cheats, thieves, liars, vagabonds, and sinful women, he set up a sort of conspiracy that would accomplish his goals. Making great promises to these people, he was able to convince them to go to great extremes for him.

Holy Scripture even relates stories that include secret, clandestine arrangements with special rendezvous and special accomplices. Two examples are the acquisition of the colt on which Jesus rode into Jerusalem on Palm Sunday, and the preparation of the Upper Room for the Last Supper.

See Mark 11:1–6. It might appear to us that Jesus somehow knew the owner of the colt, while his closest disciples did not. Schonfield suggests that Jesus would have been accompanied by hundreds of Galilean pilgrims coming to Jerusalem for the Passover feast, and just as the people of Dixon might come out and hail Ronald Reagan as special, seeing as how he would be their hometown boy made big, so likewise would these Galileans raise their voices and cry Hosanna for their hometown boy, especially if he had been able to convince his countrymen that he was a special agent of God, for much of his ministry was spent in the region of Galilee. And here he is fulfilling the prophecy of Zechariah 9:9: "Rejoice greatly O daughter of Zion! Shout aloud, O daughter of Jerusalem! Lo, your king comes to you, triumphant and victorious is he; humble and riding on an ass, on a colt the foal of an ass." Even their hosannas and chants were echoing Psalm 118. Maybe even these chants had been prearranged.

Schonfield sees the wisdom to Jesus's strategy. Not only does this make Him appear to be the messiah, but it provokes the religious leaders at a time when the show was meant to be theirs. And thus, he sets in motion the fulfillment of the prophetic vision of the Suffering Servant. (Isaiah 53).

As the plot matures, a secretive operation unfolds. It has to do with the Upper Room.

On the first day of Unleavened Bread, when the Passover lamb is sacrificed, his disciples said to him, "Where do you want us to go and make preparations for you to eat the Passover?" So, he sent two of his disciples, saying to them, "Go into the city, and a man carrying a jar of water will meet you; follow him, and wherever he enters, say to the owner of the house, 'The Teacher asks, Where is my guest room where I may eat the Passover with my disciples?' He will show you a large room upstairs, furnished and ready. Make preparations for us there" (Mark 14:12–15).

Again, we have a special unknown accomplice and a special rendezvous with whom a particular conversation is to occur to open the door for Jesus's celebration of the Passover in the Holy City. Schonfield doesn't suggest that Judas was part of the strategy. He's just a victim of circumstance, and Jesus's cause. In the plot, *they* would provoke him to turn against him the way he did. I would like it better if Judas *was* included as an instigator in the plot. Partly because I feel sorry for him, and partly because he appears a dark figure later on when he lets his guilt get the better of him, and he destroys himself.

Anyway, the next conspiracy is that of the death on the cross. Schonfield suggests that the sponge filled with vinegar was a drugged potion that would put Jesus into a deathlike trance. All was going according to plan. Jesus looked dead and yet he had to be taken down before the Sabbath began. There would be a good chance that he might be able to survive the beating and the crucifixion. That was the plan. And that was his biggest risk! Jesus believed in his messiahship so strongly that he was willing to go to great extremes himself to prove himself. But one act changes things. It was not a part of the plan. The soldier, wanting to make sure he was dead, pierced his side.

This would explain why it was so difficult for his closest disciples to recognize him after his "supposed" resurrection. It wasn't really him! And as far as the resurrection goes, Schonfield suggests that his body *was* stolen by disciples who were in on the plot. The plot that was created and perpetuated by the chief priests of Jerusalem, according to Matthew!

So, the Passover plot becomes a conspiracy for faith. People need a miracle, so let's give it to them. If it's all for the sake of faith, it can't be bad, can it? Schonfield concludes with these ideas: By his planning beyond the cross and the tomb, by his implicit confidence concerning the coming of the kingdom of God over which he was deputed to reign, Jesus had to go through to victory. The messianic program was saved from the grave of all dead hopes to become a guiding light and inspiration to the people. Wherever mankind strives to bring in the rule of justice, righteousness, and peace, there the deathless presence of Jesus the Messiah is with them. Whenever a people of God is found laboring in the cause of human brotherhood, love, and compassion, there the King of the Jews is enthroned. No other will ever come to be what He was and do what He did. The special conditions which produced him at a peculiar and pregnant moment in history are never likely to occur again. But doubtless there will be other moments having their own strange features, and other people through whom the vision will speak at an appointed time. Meanwhile we have not exhausted the potentialities of the vision of Jesus (135–36). Despite everything done to stop him in his own time and since, not only by his enemies but by his professed champions, he has continued to come through. So let no one let this presentation of Jesus Christ take notice that it is destructive of faith, or that it reveals Jesus as a deluded fanatic. If any such impression has been formed, it is very wide of the mark. What this book has aimed to reveal is that he was a man of so much faith that he dared to translate an age-old and somewhat nebulous imagination into a factual down-to-earth reality.

And so, we have the Passover plot. But what do we do with it? Do we believe it? Or do we believe the Bible? You may be wondering now, does Kingery believe it? The answer is *no*, I do not. I cannot accept the fraud it implies. I cannot accept the lies it includes. It makes Jesus out to be a false prophet, and the disciples become fools, the Gospels become a hoax, and the faith I have becomes empty in the light of the Passover plot. It eliminates any validity to true inspiration as well as to true hope.

There would be no forgiveness if there was no real sacrifice of Christ. And there would be no eternal life if there was no real resurrection. The crucifixion, death, and resurrection of Jesus are the one redeeming act that offers us salvation. There is no salvation without the grace of Christ.

I believe what the Bible says may have happened. I don't know exactly what did happen, but something amazing took place almost two thousand years ago that has changed my life today. There may be an error in taking the words of the four Gospel writers as absolute historical fact, but what was written was never meant to be history; it was meant to be scripture. It was meant to be those writings that witness to the experience of faith and that tie us together with the faith we experience.

Schonfield, in *The Passover Plot*, may be offering his witness. He tries to make sense out of something that makes no sense; namely, the rising to life of a dead man. He himself does not disqualify the whole experience of faith because of difficulty with a part of it. But some people do just that. They chuck the whole on account of a part that causes doubt.

But the important question that's raised by the issue here is what should we do with our doubt? What do we do with the questions that challenge our deeply felt beliefs?

I have seen way too many people who use their doubts as an excuse for inactivity, refusing the call to serve their neighbor, to help the poor and the needy, or to give of themselves because they are unconvinced. They have a weakened sense of commitment because they see some shortcoming in a part of the miracle.

I have seen some who reject religion entirely because there are too many types and too many denominations. They believe there is discord in the body, and they can't get it together. But who is it, really, who can't get it together? It's those people who have little or no convictions whatsoever who cannot accept a conviction of faith.

What should we do with our doubts? We should pray. We should study. Oftentimes, our doubts are due to ignorance. We just don't know the whole story. Sometimes it's only because we don't understand. But you don't need to understand an electrical current before you turn on the light. You don't need to understand the computer system or the phone company before you use a computer or call to find out good news. So likewise with faith, and with prayer, and with beliefs.

I believe in the resurrection because I believe in Jesus. I don't believe in Jesus because I believe in the resurrection. What belief in the resurrection does for me is it helps me believe that there's hope for me and for you and for a world of people who need new life. I believe in the resurrection because I believe in Jesus! Amen.

And if you want proof that Jesus never rose from death, what happened to His dead body? Or is that another part of "the plot"?

MEDITATION 23

The Big Lie

___

"While they [the two Marys] were going,
some of the guards went into the city
and told the chief priests everything that had happened.
After the priests had assembled with the elders,
they devised a plan
to give a large sum of money to the soldiers,
telling them, "You must say,
'His disciples came by night and stole him away while we were asleep.'
If this comes to the governor's ears,
we will satisfy him and keep you out of trouble."
So they took the money and did as they were directed.
And this story is still told among the Jews to this day.

—MATTHEW 28:11–15

T he two Marys had just seen Jesus, risen and alive! He had told them, "Go and tell My brothers to go to Galilee; there they will see Me!" (28:10). "While they were going, some of the guard went into the city and told the chief priests everything that had happened" (28:11).

One thing to note is that we begin to get an idea that there were obviously more than two soldiers at the tomb. "Some," to me, means more than two, and less than half of the total, otherwise it would have said "most of the guard." We don't get an exact number. The Gospels of Mark, Luke, and John don't mention any guards at all. The whole purpose of mentioning the guard detail is what comes next.

"They devised a plan ..." (v. 12). These are the supposed *righteous* leaders of the people of faith! And yet they are acting so deceitfully in the story here that it is just too impossible to believe that they would ever do such a thing. But they are acting more out of self-interest than anything else, so they are not thinking about how they are bearing false witness, and bribing the whole detail of guards to do the same. This plot is wicked from the get-go!

___

How does Mathew know about this part of the story? My guess is that either a bribed guard told them—unable to bear the guilt of this big lie—or they had someone on the inside who knew about it. I can easily imagine how at least one of the guards felt a conviction so strong after going through an earthquake, seeing the angel, and becoming aware of the reality of the resurrection that he could have come to faith in Christ. After all, there was a soldier at the foot of the cross who exclaimed, at the moment of Jesus's death: "Truly this man was the Son of God!" (27:54).

However the author discovered the truth about this big lie, it comes down through history to us. So, let's examine it for a moment. They are all bribed to say, "His Disciples came by night and stole Him away while we were asleep!" (28:13). First, let's imagine that there were ten soldiers in this guard detail. It is hard to believe that all ten fell asleep so deeply that they were able to allow anyone to sneak past them to the tomb, let alone several, or at least two of the disciples. I think two men would have been needed to carry the one dead body. Hard to believe they got past ten guards!

They had to roll the stone away from the entrance to the tomb. This would have taken at least two men. The sound of the stone being rolled away would have been loud enough to wake someone nearby! Again, making the big lie hard to believe!

Finally, if they were all sleeping, how do they know who rolled away the stone and stole the body? It's so hard to believe this big lie that it's surprising to think that anyone would ever believe it. Besides, the punishment for sleeping during guard duty would have been severe enough that no soldier worth his salt would ever be willing to admit doing so. So, let's embellish the story. Let's imagine that some of the women who had followed Christ disguised themselves as harlots and seduced their way into the midst of the guards with what they offered as "refreshment," only they were wineskins filled with something to make them sleep. However the guards were put to sleep, do you see how this lie has to now become even bigger? It's just too hard to believe!

The motive of the chief priests and the elders had been to prevent what they believed was the deception of Jesus's claim to be the Son of God from being perpetuated any further, lest "the last deception be worse than the first" (27:64). And yet their only counter to the resurrection is a lie so obvious that it reveals their desperation. Their denial of Christ is so absolute that all they can do is continue to try to discredit His name.

Even further, today, those who can't accept the truth of the resurrection will discredit Matthew and all the Gospel writers because Matthew is the only one who says anything about the guards, and, since the other Gospels don't mention it, then Matthew must be embellishing his story. Therefore, it must not be true. That means Matthew must have lied; therefore his whole story must be false; therefore all the Gospels are false; therefore Christianity is false!

Do you see how this lie must keep growing even bigger? If Matthew is lying about the lies of the chief priests and Pharisees, then maybe the guards never did receive a bribe, never did tell a lie, they never even existed anyway, and then the disciples never stole the body of Christ! And yet, Matthew says, "This story is told among the Jews to this day!" (Matthew 28:15).

For the resurrection to be false, the body of Christ must have been stolen! And yet look at what has happened. Christianity has grown, mission work is being done, ministry is being offered, millions of dollars support this work; love, kindness, hope, and joy are all spreading from generation to generation. Souls are being saved. The kingdom is being preached. And the church lives on!

How could all this be the result of a lie?

Even if it is a lie, we still must choose between lies!

Either the resurrection is real, or they really stole the body! Which reality makes more sense to you?

The Great Truth and the Big Lie (Continued)

THE GREAT TRUTH

I t is glorious to believe. Just in the thought of the resurrection is glory! There is a hope. There is a power. It cannot be denied. Because of the resurrection, His disciples could proclaim that Jesus is Lord; Jesus is the Son of God; Jesus is the Messiah, the Christ! A wonderful fire begins to burn in the hearts of believers. The resurrection of Jesus did something remarkable for those who first experienced this great truth. It made them bold enough to proclaim their experience, their understanding of the promises of the kingdom of God, the truth of grace, and the triumph of faith. It happened just less than two thousand years ago, but the truth, this great truth, is still as fresh today as if Jesus had risen this morning!

The resurrection does something for us!

Just as Christ was raised from the dead by the glory of the Father, so we too might walk in newness of life. For if we have been united with Him in a death like His, we will certainly be united with Him in a resurrection like His. We know that our old self was crucified with Him so that the body of sin might be destroyed, and we might no longer be enslaved to sin. For whoever has died is freed from sin. But if we have died with Christ, we believe that we will also live with Him. We know that Christ, being raised from the dead, will never die again; death no longer has dominion over Him. The death He died, He died to sin, once for all; but the life He lives, He lives to God. So, you also must consider yourselves dead to sin and alive to God in Christ Jesus. Therefore, do not let sin exercise dominion in your mortal bodies to make you obey their passions. No longer present your members to sin as instruments of wickedness, but present yourselves to God as those who have been brought from death to life, and present your members to God as instruments of righteousness. For sin will have no dominion over you, since you are not under law but under grace! (Romans 6:4b–14).

The resurrection changes us!

> It is God who said, "Let light shine out of darkness," who has shone in our hearts to give the light of knowledge of the glory of God in the face of Jesus Christ. But we have this treasure in earthen vessels, so that it may be made clear that this extraordinary power belongs to God and does not come from us. We are afflicted in every way, but not crushed; perplexed, but not driven to despair; persecuted, but not forsaken; struck down, but not destroyed; always carrying in the body the death of Jesus so that the life of Jesus may also be made visible in our bodies. (2 Corinthians 4:6–10)

The resurrection inspires us!

The Word is near you, on your lips and in your heart, (that is, the word of faith that we proclaim); because if you confess with your lips that Jesus is Lord and believe in your heart that God raised Him from the dead, you will be saved. For one believes with the heart and so is justified, and one confesses with the mouth and so is saved! (Romans 10:6–10)

The resurrection comforts us! It gives us hope. There is a faithful way of seeing our own deaths as a new beginning!

> Just as we have borne the image of the man of dust, we will also bear the image of the man of heaven. When this perishable body puts on imperishability, and this mortal body puts on immortality, then the saying that is written will be fulfilled: "Death has been swallowed up in victory." Where, O death, is your victory? Where, O death, is your sting?

The sting of death is sin, and the power of sin is the law. But thanks be to God who gives us the victory through our Lord Jesus Christ!
—1 Corinthians 15:49, 54–57

The resurrection reveals a glorious power for healing!

If the Spirit of Him who raised Jesus from the dead dwells in you, He who raised Christ from the dead will give life to your mortal bodies also through His Spirit that dwells in you! I consider that the sufferings of this present time are not worth comparing with the glory about to be revealed to us! (Romans 8:11, 18)

The resurrection gives us a whole new way of looking at life! It's as if we can see the world through new lenses. We gain perfect vision! "When the perfect comes, the imperfect will pass away!" (1Corinthians 13:10). Look at Second Corinthians 5:14–17:

The love of Christ urges us on, because we are convinced that one has died for all; therefore all have died. And He died for all, so that those who live might live no longer for themselves, but for Him who died and was raised for them. From now on, therefore, we regard no one from a human point of view; even though we once knew Christ from a human point of view, we know Him no longer in this way. So if anyone is in Christ, there is a new creation: everything old has passed away; behold, everything has become new!

The resurrection is a wonderful sign of grace!

God, who is rich in mercy, out of the great love with which He loved us even when we were dead through our trespasses, made us alive together with Christ—by grace you have been saved—and raised us up with Him and seated us with Him in the heavenly places in Christ Jesus so that in the ages to come He might show the immeasurable riches of His grace in kindness toward us in Christ Jesus! (Ephesians 2:4–7)

The resurrection reveals something wonderfully transcendent! The way of the world is eclipsed by this great truth. The things of earth are overshadowed by the surpassing wonder of what God has done in Christ! Jesus even said, "In the world you will have trouble; but take courage, I have overcome the world!" (John 16:33). Not only do we rise above the imperfection of this world by faith in Jesus, we can be triumphant! Theologians and scholars have said that the resurrection proves that Jesus is Lord, that Jesus is the Son of God, that Jesus is the Messiah, the King, the ruler of creation. And because of this we should therefore not only believe in Jesus, but we should heed His teaching.

But still, it takes faith to acknowledge that the resurrection is true, real, factual. It takes trust in the testimony of the first witnesses. In Mark's Gospel, the disciples just didn't believe Mary Magdalene when she told them she had seen Jesus alive (16:11). Later though, Mark tells that Jesus, when He appeared to all of them personally, "rebuked them for their lack of faith and stubborn refusal to believe her testimony" (16:14). In Luke, the disciples did not believe the women, because their words seemed to them like an idle tale! (24:11). But in Luke, Peter went to see the tomb. He had to see it for himself. Even in the Gospel of John, they had to see for themselves (20:3–9). When Thomas, who doubted so severely at first, finally came to believe, Jesus said to him, "Because you have seen me, you believe? Blessed are those who have not seen and yet have believed!" (20:29). And that's me! That's us! We believe because we trust the witness of all who have gone before us who believed, who experienced the resurrection's power and glory!

But if Jesus did not rise from the dead, they have all been fooled! Paul said:

If Christ has not been raised, then our proclamation has been in vain and your faith has been in vain. We are even found to be misrepresenting God, because we testify of

God that He raised Christ (whom He did not raise if it is true that the dead are not raised)! For if the dead are not raised, then Christ has not been raised. If Christ has not been raised, your faith is futile and you are still in your sins. Then those also who have died in Christ have perished. If for this life only we have hoped in Christ, we are of all people most to be pitied. (1 Corinthians 15:14–19)

THE BIG LIE

The idea of the resurrection is, for the more worldly minded, too good to be true. It doesn't make sense. It is foolish. But the message of the cross makes sense in the light of the resurrection! "The message of the Cross is foolishness to those who are perishing, but to us who are being saved it is the power of God!" (1 Corinthians 1:18). And Paul said, "God's foolishness is wiser than human wisdom, and God's weakness is stronger than human strength!" (1:25).

If the idea of the resurrection is just too good to be true, there are also some who simply deny or reject it. Some people are always looking for reasons not to believe. They do so in order not to have to change their lives or their way of thinking, let alone let their lives be changed by God. In the Gospel of Matthew, one reason not to believe, or, to deny it, part of what you could call the great lie, is the idea that the disciples stole Jesus's body out of the tomb to make it look as though He had been raised! But if this is true, then a whole religion, a whole worldview, a whole system of belief is based on a lie! It would be the same if the "swoon" theory was accepted. That's the idea that Jesus never really died. He fainted, awoke in the coolness of the tomb, and made it appear as if He had been raised. This is part of what nonbelievers call the "Passover plot." Another part of the great lie is the idea that the disciples were mistaken. They went to the wrong tomb, and it was empty. If they are not mistaken, then they fabricated the idea of the resurrection to create the illusion that Jesus was something more than human. They pretended He was the Messiah, the Lord. And they did it so well that they convinced others to believe it, and that belief has perpetuated a myth or legend.

But the resurrection of Jesus has such a power to it that it lives. We are here today because of the power of the resurrection! The teachings of Christ and of His followers over the centuries have created almost two thousand years of charity through mission, ministry, and service. We can all acknowledge that many injustices have been done in the name of Christ down through the ages, but there is more hope in the world, more goodness done, more grace proclaimed because of believers than if Christ had never been raised and the church had never existed.

Let's go back to Romans 6. Paul had spoken about the issue of baptism. Starting at verse 4b, he said: "Just as Christ was raised from the dead by the glory of the Father, so we too might walk in newness of life. For if we have been united with Him in a death like His, we will certainly be united with Him in a resurrection like His." Then, beginning at verse 8, he says: "If we have died with Christ, we believe that we will also live with Him. We know that Christ, being raised from the dead, will never die again; death no longer has dominion over Him. The death he died, he died to sin, once for all; but the life he lives, he lives to God. So you also must reckon yourselves dead to sin, and alive to God in Christ Jesus" (8–11).

When Paul says "reckon," he does not mean that the act of "reckoning" something creates a new entity, (even if he did, that would still mean that the Christian who had thus "reckoned" was already alive the other side of death); the language of "reckoning" is that of adding up a sum, a column of figures. When I add up the money in my bank account, that does not create the money; life is not, alas, that easy. It merely informs me of the amount that is already there. When I have completed the "reckoning," I have not brought about a new state of affairs in the real world outside my mind; the only new state of affairs is that my mind is now aware of the way things really are.

So, it is here. When Paul says in verse 4 that "as the Messiah was raised from the dead through the Father's glory, so also are we to walk in newness of life," he is not asking of Christians something that being still "dead" they are unable to perform (N. T. Wright, The Resurrection of the Christ, part 2, 252). And then, Paul says, "Present yourselves to God as alive from the dead, and your members as instruments of righteousness to God" (v. 13). Telling someone to present themselves to God, when they are not in any sense "alive from the dead," is like telling someone to leap from a high building "as if you had wings" when they do not. Paul's strong ethical argument, then, is not simply that there are two ways to live, and that one must choose between them; it is that the baptized person has changed their ground and must learn to behave according to the territory in which they now find themselves (Ibid; 253).

The resurrection has changed everything! It changes our lives. It changes the way we look at the world. The resurrection is a power, the power of grace, of love, of forgiveness, of new life, of truth!

A great truth!

You Can't Stop Them Now!

While they were going,
some of the guard went into the city and told the chief priests everything that had happened.
After the priests had assembled with the elders,
they devised a plan to give a large sum of money to the soldiers,
telling them, "You must say,
'His disciples came by night and stole him away while we were asleep.'
If this comes to the governor's ears,
we will satisfy him and keep you out of trouble."
So they did as they were directed.
And this story is still told among the Jews to this day.

Now the eleven disciples went to Galilee,
to the mountain to which Jesus had directed them.
When they saw him, they worshiped him;
but some doubted.
And Jesus came to them and said to them,
"All authority in heaven and earth has been given to me.
Go therefore and make disciples of all nations,
baptizing them in the name of the Father and of the Son and of the Holy Spirit,
and teaching them to obey everything I have commanded you.
And remember, I am with you always,
to the end of the age."

—MATTHEW 28:11–20

Yes, Caiaphas, I have paid the guards. I paid them grandly. They will tell everyone that they all fell asleep. As hard as that will be to believe, they will also tell everyone that while they were unaware, his disciples came and stole his body to make it look like he had risen from the dead. And I told them that we will defend them to Pilate if he becomes a problem. At least, there will have been no uprisings during the Passover Feast, for that he will be glad. But Caiaphas, we still have a problem. We need to produce the dead body of this man.

The story is absurd, Caiaphas! Not just because they must convince everyone that they all fell asleep, but that none of them were awakened by the removing of the stone that closed off the entrance to the tomb. Caiaphas, we cannot delay. The longer we wait to act, to prove to the world that this pretender is dead, that he did not rise from death, the easier it will be for people to believe in him.

No, Caiaphas, it would be impossible to suggest to Pilate, or to the people, that the conspiracy of a resurrection included the temple guards. They have all, to a man, proven their loyalty to the High Priesthood many times over. Everyone would know that. That is why I chose each of them to guard the tomb.

They said there was an earthquake. Did you feel anything? I did not! They said they saw an angel, Caiaphas, have you ever seen an angel? Neither have I … I don't think. But Caiaphas, they said something blinded them, something brilliant, like lightning. They said it was the angel, that his raiment was white as snow. And they were all so terrified that they were paralyzed, scared stiff.

Some women had even seen them. The women had come to the tomb at dawn to honor their teacher. This, I understand. This is only natural, only practical. But the women did not become useless. They were filled with joy, while the guards all around them were frozen in terror, trembling, not in awe, but in raw fear. I imagine, Caiaphas, that the way they saw it, and the way the women saw it must have been completely different.

Caiaphas, we could try to discredit those women, say they were possessed by demons, and that they were so wicked that they poisoned the guards with their very scent to put them to sleep! Sorceresses! Witches! Caiaphas, we could try to tell everyone that they were witches!

No. No, that would not work. Too many people have known them for too long. Even you and I have known what they were like, and look at what they have become. They are hailed as good women by even the best of the Sanhedrin. We could not create any false testimony against Jesus the other night from any who might have said he had turned people into sinners.

We, the scribes and the Pharisees, were the only ones Jesus angered. We were the only ones he called sinners. Caiaphas, it is so hard to create a lie. It is so hard to say anything against this man! Too many have been blessed by his healing powers, by his kindness, by his forgiveness, by his love!

Rumor has it that the disciples have gone to Galilee. They are taking the body of Jesus to his own back yard. If he gets there, they will have more places to hide him than we have people to search. Caiaphas! We must use haste. We can't let rumors of a resurrection take root. We cannot let such an idea give this man's name any sense of credibility. Without a dead body, or, with the notion that He still lives, we will look foolish, for he will have proven himself to have been at least something of what he said he was. Any man that can suffer what he suffered, any man who can endure what he endured, any man who can seem to be so absolutely dead and still live will prove to be much more than a mere man!

Caiaphas, consider this … What if we are unable to expose their plot to make the man look as if God *had* raised him up from death? They will all remember how he had proclaimed that in three days he would rise! They will think Him much more than a mere teacher, much more than a heater, much more than a rebel. They will think of him with the status of a prophet, and perhaps, Caiaphas, they will think of him, since it was his claim, to be the Messiah! Then what will become of us?

Caiaphas, if we do not produce Jesus of Nazareth dead as soon as possible, we will lose the opportunity to disprove his claim to be the son of God. Because of their belief in his resurrection, many are already calling themselves followers of Christ! His reputation will spread like fire! His following will increase! People will be so enthralled with "the man who died and was raised" that his teachings will spread. His way of humility and sacrificial love will become more popular than the Law! His teaching will gain not only a certain credibility, but a popularity, an authority, a life of their own! And remember how he taught people about us Pharisees. What will become of our reputation?

The idea that he has risen will give him a power we never anticipated. It will give his reforms a legitimacy we could not tolerate. It will give his spirit an all-pervasive immanence that they will claim that he is somehow with them always. You can't stop them now, Caiaphas! Not unless we defeat his following right away. Not even Elijah had such a hold on people. Not even Moses had such an effect. This Jesus will forever be an annoying nuisance for us, Caiaphas.

I, Saul of Tarsus, am at your disposal. Send me now, and I will arrest them all as blasphemers. Send me now and I will bring them bound to

Jerusalem. I will make a spectacle of them in such a way that they will regret what they have done. They will regret having believed in Jesus. They will regret having stolen his body to make it look as if He had been raised from death. They will regret even knowing the name of Jesus.

But first, Caiaphas, we must prove that He did not rise from death. And the only way to do that is to find his dead body. Caiaphas, I will go to Galilee if it is your will. If his body is there, I will find it. If not, I will go anywhere I think it may be. Caiaphas, I would even go to Damascus! We must find the dead body of Jesus of Nazareth, or he will surely become to the world Jesus the Christ!

The body of Jesus has never been found. The Body of Christ still lives. The power of His presence is here in our hearts. And the power of His resurrection is proven by the change in the lives of many peoples, not the least of which was the life of Saul of Tarsus. You may know him better as Paul the apostle.

Kingdom, Power, and Glory

Then David blessed the Lord in the presence of all the assembly;
David said:
"Blessed are you, O Lord, the God of our ancestor Israel, forever and ever.
Yours, O Lord, are the greatness, the power, the glory, the victory, and the majesty;
for all that is in the heavens and on the earth is yours;
yours is the kingdom, O Lord,
and you are exalted as head above all.
Riches and honor come from you, and you rule over all.
In your hand are power and might;
and it is in your hand to make great and to give strength to all.
And now, our God, we give thanks to you and praise your glorious name.

—1 CHRONICLES 29:10–13

He said to me,
"My grace is sufficient for you,
for power is made perfect in weakness."
So I will boast all the more gladly of my weaknesses,
so that the power of Christ may dwell in me.

—2 CORINTHIANS 12:9

Now the eleven disciples went to Galilee,
to the mountain to which Jesus had directed them.
When they saw him, they worshiped him;
but some doubted.
And Jesus came to them and said to them,
"All authority in heaven and on earth has been given to me.
Go therefore and make disciples of all nations,
baptizing them in the name of the Father and of the Son and of the Holy Spirit,
and teaching them to obey everything that I have commanded you.
And remember, I am with you always, to the end of the age."

—MATTHEW 28:16–20

After Thorvaldsen had completed his famous statue of Christ, he brought a friend to see it. Christ's arms were outstretched, His head bowed between them. The friend criticized the work by saying that from wherever he stood, he could not see the face of Christ. "Yes," the sculptor replied. "If you would see the face of Christ, you must get down on your knees."

It seems that worshiping on our knees is one way of being humble before the divine presence of God. I've been heard saying that, in prayer, we present ourselves to the presence of God. There is no perfect position and no perfect method to do so, but the suggestion offered by Thorvaldsen evokes the necessity of prayer to see Christ face to face.

I would only want to briefly urge that prayer could be a way of being with God in the world. We need it. Sometimes, it seems, we need it more and more each year as we propel ourselves deeper into the pace of technological velocity. Personally, prayer is one of the many things that hold me more accountable to God's heavenly kingdom, and my service for its sake. It is for the sake of the kingdom that we pray, even when we pray for our own needs, because we too are children of the kingdom, and to serve our Lord, we must have our needs met, both spiritual and physical. The kingdom is our destiny and our purpose. We seek it, and we serve it now. The place of prayer in anyone's life is important, for it can determine the place of the soul in the kingdom of God. Without prayer, and the proper attitude toward living, loving, and the personal enhancement of our relationships with God, others, and even with ourselves, we are more likely to be humanists than true Christians. The prayers we offer are the songs of the kingdom.

THINE IS THE KINGDOM

And there is a kingdom known only by the heart. It has no beginning, no end, no castles, and no borders. There is no wall about it to keep anyone in or out. It is led to by no roads, but there is a Way, and it's approached by a journey. But the journey is not necessarily one that takes us any great distance, for this kingdom is reached by the pilgrimage of faith. The kingdom is nowhere, yet it is everywhere. It is a kingdom not to be seen, but it can be felt. It cannot be displayed, but it can be witnessed. It is a kingdom that does not conquer, and yet it draws all nations into its realm. Its conqueror was a victim; his kingdom is a kingdom of kindness, a kingdom of peace, a kingdom of salvation and of reconciliation, a kingdom of redemption, of freedom, and, a kingdom of service. It's a kingdom where all become equal, and yet all become servants; it's a kingdom of the spirit, and yet it still serves the flesh. It's a kingdom of goodness, it's a kingdom of love.

Thine is the kingdom, O God; Thine is the throne.

THINE IS THE POWER

There is a power that is known in this kingdom. It does not destroy, but it does make things new; it makes things change. It does not defeat, but it does claim a victory. It is a power we feel, and yet it is not ours. It is a power we hold, and yet it is not our own. It holds us and works in us and through us. For the power is weakness and folly to the world. It wears no armor but spiritual armor; it wields no weapon but spiritual weapons; this power is seen in submission, and it's whispered in worship. Its force is made greater the more it is used. Its effect is its cause. For it's a power that draws from the efforts of faith. It comes from the source of our spirits, our souls, and it touches our flesh and inspires our minds. It teaches us to be still, and it compels us to move. It lays down our lives, and it lifts us to God.

Thine is the power, O God. Thine is the might!

THINE IS THE GLORY

And there is a glory that is brought by this power. It's a glory that is humble, awarded no earthly crown. It comes as a treasure, and yet it cannot be counted. It is known in a victory that comes to the heart. It's a feeling of triumph unboastingly silent. It is praise that is offered for a beauty that's beyond what is seen. It is lifted in song, and it bows down our heads. This glory is given as a blessing for the hopeless, and yet it's a hope that brings trust in God's mercy. For it's a glory of death that brings life eternal.

And Thine is the glory, O God. Thine is the praise.

FOREVER

And there is a time we know that never begins, yet it happens around us, within us, and through us without ceasing. We call it "forever" because it is now, and it feels eternal. It seems without end in days or in miles. And it carries on after we've met all our limitations. Forever, eternity, the fulfillment of time, another dimension, beyond mortal thought. Forever is now, and forever is after. It comes from before, sometimes, it comes from tomorrow. But forever is always—world without end.

AMEN.

The heart says "Amen" to the words that we pray, when we pray them sincerely. It is as it's said when said as the truth. So be it.

Thine is the kingdom, the power, and the glory, forever. Amen!

The Lord's Prayer, in the sixth chapter of Matthew, seems so unfinished as it is presented. And so, a doxology attached through tradition is added when we pray its words to round it all out. The words are familiar as if taken from the prayer of David offered at the end of his life for the beginning of the building of the temple in Jerusalem.

Thine is the kingdom. The emphasis belongs to God. The kingdom is for us to enter, but it belongs to God. The bridge that opens the kingdom to us is determined for our crossing by the relationships we have. Human to human as well as human to divine.

The bridge is built at first by doing God's will on earth. Not by doing it as we choose but doing it as it is done in heaven. Second, the bridge is built by forgiveness: And God forgives us our trespasses as we forgive those who have trespassed against us.

Thine is the power. The power of faith is not ours. Faith is not *our* power, but God's. And the way this power is shown is in love. And love is something that serves rather than demands, as some forms of power seem to do. It encourages rather than boasts.

Love brings grace and growth rather than law and limitations. Paul, himself, bears witness to the power of grace, for through Paul, God's power was made perfect in weakness. In 1 Corinthians 2:1–5 Paul says:

When I came to you, I did not come proclaiming to you the testimony of God in lofty words or wisdom. For I decided to know nothing among you except Jesus Christ and him crucified. And I was with you in weakness and in much fear and trembling; and my speech and my message were not in plausible words of wisdom but in demonstration of the spirit of power, that your faith might rest not in the wisdom of mortals, but in the power of God.

Faith is a divine power that is working through us. In the New Testament, there are two words for power. One is *exousia*, which is the force of authority; and the other is *dunamis*, from which is derived the word *dynamo* or *dynamite*.

There were occasions when Christ bore witness to the dynamo of God's power within himself as he was able to heal and perform other miracles. And there were occasions when Christ expressed the authority even to forgive sins. In his final commission to his disciples in the Gospel of Matthew, the risen Jesus said: "All authority in heaven and on earth has been given to me." And because of this, this power, the disciples were all the more able to compel people by their witness to become followers of Jesus, making disciples in the name of the Father and of the Son and of the Holy Spirit, "And Lo," because of this power, Christ said, "I am with you always."

And thine is the glory. Jesus prayed not to be saved from the hour of his sacrifice.

"No, for this purpose I have come to this hour. Father, glorify your name." Then a voice came from heaven that said, "I have glorified it! And I will glorify it again!" The crowd standing by heard the voice, and some said that it had thundered. Others thought an angel had spoken to him. Then Jesus said, "This voice has come for your sake, not for mine. Now is the judgment of this world, now shall the ruler of this world be cast out; and I, when I am lifted up from the earth, will draw all men to myself" (John 12:27–32).

And Jesus still draws people to himself. This is affirmed when people celebrate their faith in the church, by joining the church, by serving their Lord, and by doing God's will. They are drawn, not to a building, not to a preacher, not to a fellowship, for all those things are there for the purpose of glorifying God's name. And it has all happened because when Jesus was lifted up, his sacrifice became the grace that draws people to him. And even as the whole world seemed to begin to know that Jesus was the Christ, crying "hosanna" in his honor, Jesus said, "The hour has come for the Son of Man to be glorified." And then he began to talk of his death: "Truly, truly, I say unto you, unless a grain of wheat falls to the earth and dies, it remains alone; but if it dies, it bears much fruit. He who loves his life loses it, and he who hates his life in this world will keep it for eternal life." And rather than praying for God to save his life, he prayed for God to glorify his name. And so, God is glorified as His son dies, and He died to live again, to be raised, proving the power of God, manifesting the kingdom of faith, giving life eternal to all who believed.

Thine is the kingdom and the power and the glory forever. Eternally, without end either in time or in space, for the kingdom is for all people, and the power is for the love that it inspires.

Thine is the kingdom and the power and the glory forever. Amen.

Truly. It is as it's said when it's said as the truth.

Amen.

PART 3
The Resurrection in Mark

Here is a part of my "gallery" that comes between the separate wings of Matthew and Luke. It is a short hallway with just enough space for several portraits of the resurrection message from Mark. The story Mark tells is virtually the same as Matthew's and Luke's, though there are still very minor differences. Of particular relevance is that the women don't tell anyone about their experience! (at least in the first ending of Mark). And there are special "additions" to Mark that are very different in both the experience of those who first testified to the resurrection and the feeling of the story (particularly the notions of snake-handling and the immunity to poisons). Though I don't go there, the scenes that receive my focus simply seemed relevant to share. Again, it is all very inspiring.

The Empty Tomb

When the sabbath was over,
Mary Magdalene, and Mary the mother of James, and Salome bought spices,
so that they might go and anoint him.
And very early on the first day of the week,
when the sun had risen, they went to the tomb. They had been saying to one another,
"Who will roll away the stone for us
from the entrance to the tomb?"
When they looked up, they saw that the stone, which was very large,
had already been rolled back.
As they entered the tomb,
they saw a young man, dressed in a white robe, sitting on the right side;
and they were alarmed.
But he said to them, "Do not be alarmed;
you are looking for Jesus of Nazareth,
who was crucified.
He has been raised; he is not here.
Look, there is the place they laid him.
But go, tell his disciples and Peter
that he is going ahead of you to Galilee;
there you will see him, just as he told you."
So they went out and fled from the tomb,
for terror and amazement had seized them;
and they said nothing to anyone,
for they were afraid.

—MARK 16:1–8

Martin Buber tells the story of Rabbi Eisik of Cracow, the capital of Poland, who had a dream in which a voice told him to journey to Prague, where under the great bridge to the royal castle he would discover a hidden treasure. He finally decided to go—making the journey by foot. Now, legend tells that Polish rabbis are very wise. As Rabbi Eisik approached one village on his way to Prague, he caught up with two men just outside of town, dragging a buck by its hind legs to take it to the village butcher. He could see that they were exhausted and suggested that it might be a lot easier if they dragged the buck by his antlers, and then he went on ahead of them into the village. Rabbi Eisik stopped at the kosher butcher shop to purchase some food for himself, and he told the butcher that there would soon be two men with a buck coming to his shop. They were just outside of town, so he suggested that the butcher might want to assist them and that for his efforts he might get paid. Well, the butcher ran out to the edge of town, and the men were nowhere in sight. Never trust a rabbi on a journey, he said to himself.

Meanwhile, after about half an hour of dragging the buck by the antlers, one man said to the other, "That rabbi was right. This sure is a lot easier." "Yes," said the other, "but don't you think we should be going in the other direction?"

Well, I don't know if they ever made it to town, but Rabbi Eisik continued to Prague. On arriving, he easily found the bridge; but as there were armed sentinels posted there day and night, he did not venture to dig. But day after day, he returned and loitered around trying to study the situation. Finally, he attracted the attention of one of the guards. "Have you lost anything, my good man?" asked the guard. The rabbi told him of his dream. The officer laughed and exclaimed, "You poor man, to have worn out a pair of shoes traveling all this way because of a dream! Why, I had a foolish dream once myself. A voice commanded me to go to Cracow in Poland and search for a Rabbi Eisik, where I would find a great treasure buried in a dirty corner behind the stove. Imagine believing in such a dream!" And he laughed again, loud and long.

Hiding his joy, Rabbi Eisik bowed politely and bid the officer farewell. He then hurriedly journeyed back to Cracow. There, he dug under the neglected corner behind the stove, and found the treasure—thus putting an end to his poverty and finding a whole new life for himself.

Three women journeyed to the tomb of Christ on the first day of the week. They were looking for the body of a dead man, but they found something new, something strange, something awesome. It was amazing: The tomb was empty. It was so amazing that it seems they couldn't even speak. And this angel said, "Do not be alarmed!" Do not be alarmed!?

Are you kidding? Jesus Christ has risen from death, and we should not be alarmed? The world has suddenly turned upside down, and we should not be alarmed! Something has happened that really matters. A new creation has occurred; the tomb was empty. "Behold, I am about to create new heavens and a new earth!" (Isaiah 65:17a). A whole new way of looking at the world has just arrived! A new way of understanding life! A new way even of looking at death! After this, dying takes on a whole new meaning. "And the former things shall not be remembered or come to mind!" (Isaiah 65:17b).

Paul said: "The last enemy to be destroyed is death!" (1 Corinthians 15:26). And the tomb was empty! He was not there! Jesus had risen! Death was defeated! Christ is the conqueror and ours is the victory! "For as in Adam all die, so also in Christ shall all be made alive!" (1 Corinthians 15:22). And in Revelation, the consuming vision is in chapter 20: "And the sea gave up the dead in it, Death and Hades gave up the dead in them, and all were judged by what they had done. Then Death and Hades were thrown into the lake of fire" (Revelation 20:13–14).

The last enemy to be defeated is death. What does it mean to you that in Christ resurrection is death's defeat? The tomb was empty! Death has a new meaning! And because of this, all of life has a new meaning. Just as for Eisik of Cracow, discovering that the new life he sought had been right there all along, we too can know the difference just by digging into the corners of our own lives, and there, we'll find Christ. By faith we are in Christ and Christ is in us. By faith! In 2 Corinthians, Paul said: "If anyone is in Christ, they are a new creation; the old has passed away, behold, the new has come!" (5:17). Let me share the verses that lead up to those wonderful words:

> The love of Christ controls us (it happens by having Christ
> in us), because we are convinced that one has died for all,
> therefore all have died. And he died for all that those who
> live might live no longer for themselves (the old way has
> passed away), but for him who for their sake died and was
> raised. From now on therefore, we regard no one from a
> human point of view. ... Therefore, if anyone is in Christ,
> they are a new creation!" (2 Corinthians 5:13–17)

The resurrection is not just an event that happened sometime in the past. Rabbi Eisik experienced a resurrection of sorts. So did the hunters dragging the buck (believe it or not). We can too! And it's not something that might happen in some unknown future; it is the power of becoming a new creation, it is here and now, today, and tomorrow. The message of Christianity is that there is a new reality. A new way of looking at and understanding the world. It appeared long ago, do not be amazed, it still appears. It seems hidden, but it's here; it seems far away, but it's within you—if you believe. Accept it; enter into it; let it grasp you. You are a new creation. The old has passed away; behold, the new has come. The door has been opened, never to be shut again. Come on in!

Yes, the old has passed away, but sometimes it still haunts us. Jesus was raised, but he still had scars. Still, something has happened that really matters. Jesus told the Pharisees that they were "like whitewashed tombs, which outwardly appear beautiful, but within they are full of dead men's bones and all uncleanness" (Matthew 23:27). People all around us are dying inside! They can't find the treasure that's buried in some long-neglected corner. Mary Magdalene, Mary the mother of James, and Salome were looking for a dead man's bones. But the tomb was empty! Does Jesus Christ rise from within you, or are you dying inside?

We all look fine on the outside; anyone can put up a good front, but on the inside, we need resurrection. Don't leave Jesus buried in your heart, let Him rise; let Him have the power that's already His, then, "Before you call, God will answer, while you are yet speaking, he will hear" (Isaiah 65:24). The world will change. Let Christ be the real power of your faith. Don't just "have" faith, as if it were buried inside. The difference is that Christ arose. I want to come to you and find that the tomb is empty; Christ rises from within you. You're not dying inside.

If anyone is in Christ, they *are* a new creation! If anyone is in Christ, they are a *new creation!* If anyone *is* in Christ, *they* are a new creation!

Do not be alarmed!

Rolled Away

"They said nothing to anyone … because they were afraid!"
—MARK 16:8B

They were in shock. They were disoriented. They didn't know how to react. They just ran away!

On Friday, just before sunset, Mary Magdalene and Mary the mother of James watched from a distance as they saw Joseph of Arimathea take the body of Jesus, wrap it in a linen shroud, and bury it in a tomb cut out of the rock. Joseph was a prominent member of the Sanhedrin. Not a typical Pharisee, he was one who felt a distinctive hope, an inspired expectation, a longing for God's fulfillment of His divine plans. Mark describes him as one who was "waiting for the Kingdom of God" (15:43). In the Gospel of John, he is described as "a disciple of Jesus, but secretly because he feared the Jews" (John 19:29). Joseph had a unique appreciation for Jesus among his peers. And so, out of the deepest respect, he honored Jesus by giving Him an informal and humble yet reverential burial.

Now it is Sunday morning. No work could be done on the Sabbath—sunset Friday to sunset Saturday—and yet the conversation among a few of the women must have been concerned with what had been left undone in the hasty entombment of their Master, their Healer, their Savior. The body of Jesus had not been anointed, as far as they knew. (According to John 19:39–40, it had been anointed). So, with the help of Salome, the two Marys made it their first priority to do so as soon as it was light.

Their eyes were fixed on the path ahead since the sun had barely risen and the darkness of night still lingered. The sky was brightening but the shadows were still dark on earth. They spoke quietly to each other—the two Marys leading the way. A realization began to dawn on them as they pictured their destination. A great stone had been rolled against the entrance to the tomb. "Who will roll away the stone?" (v. 3).

How many times have you heard the expression, "We'll cross that bridge when we get there." On they went. Nothing deterred them from their task. Perhaps they thought they could enlist a few strong men, as they passed nearby, to come to their aid. But when they came within sight of the tomb and glanced up from their path, they felt a curious sense of surprise. God was just getting them warmed up. "The stone, which was very large, had been rolled away!" (v. 4). It must have given them pause, at first. They didn't worry about who or how, they just felt relieved. Though I'm sure they must have wondered—When did *this* happen?

Not commonly thought of as a miracle that the stone had been rolled away, partly because it was humanly possible for several men to do so, and incredibly minor beside the awesome next discovery, that stone stood as both a hindrance and a safeguard. As a safeguard, it would protect the dead body from those who might intend evil. But for Mary Magdalene, Mary the mother of James, and Salome, the stone would have been a hindrance, keeping them from coming to Christ.

And so, I ask, what are the stones in this world that might keep you from coming to Christ, from coming all the way? Is there any doubt or inability to trust? Do you doubt the fantastic quality of the story? Are you unable to trust the testimony of twenty centuries of believers? Could there be a stone that needs to be rolled away from your heart before you can completely come to Christ? Is there some inward barrier that makes you hold back? Is it fear? Fear of what you might have to do if you gave yourself over to the whole truth, the Holy truth?

"As they entered the tomb, they saw a young man dressed in a white robe sitting on the right side" (v. 5). Now their sense of surprise surely began to swell. "They were alarmed!" They were shocked. They were speechless. They came expecting to anoint the lifeless body of their Lord, and instead they encounter this messenger who appeared as a young man. I imagine his demeanor to have been calm and passive, and his voice to have been gentle, almost soothing.

"Do not be alarmed; you are looking for Jesus of Nazareth, who was crucified. He has been raised; He is not here. Look, there is the place they laid Him. But go, tell His disciples and Peter that He is going ahead of you to Galilee; there you will see Him, just as He told you" (vv. 6–7).

The rising swell of surprise turned into shock and confusion. In part, it may have been that the presence of this unknown "man" startled them. It may have been his appearance that left them stunned. But more than anything, that Jesus was not even there may have paralyzed them a bit. And then to hear that He had risen and that He is going to Galilee, "there you will find Him!" They were not just thrown into shock; they were traumatized.

That's why they ran "trembling and bewildered." And it is only in Mark that they said nothing to anyone. They were afraid. Finally, out of breath, only a few hundred yards away, as I imagine the scene, I see them stop where they felt safe again. No one else was around. They got a grip on themselves; worried, disoriented, still speechless, they go into the home of Salome—maybe she lived in Jerusalem—and they sit, crying, embracing each other, composing each other, still full of fear, and yet, I imagine one of them—for me it's Mary Magdalene—feeling the beginnings of awareness rise within.

How does your imagination fill in the gaps in the story?

"He is risen," she says, almost as if it was a question, almost as if finally saying it out loud might take her fear away. She says it again and begins to smile. "He is risen!" The other two say it. They begin to smile. A new feeling begins to replace their fear and shock. It is joy. Now, they have a different reason to catch their breath!

The stone was rolled away!

At first, because they were afraid, they said nothing to anyone. In time, in a short time, I believe, they weren't afraid anymore! "*Go, tell His disciples and Peter, 'He is going ahead of you to Galilee. You'll see Him there!'*"

"We'll see Him there!" Christ is risen! The stone was rolled away!

Stubborn Refusal

Now after he rose early on the first day of the week,
he appeared first to Mary Magdalene,
from whom he had cast out seven demons.
She went out and told those who had been with him,
while they were mourning and weeping.
But when they heard that he was alive and had been seen by her,
they would not believe it.
After this he appeared in another form to two of them,
as they were walking into the country.
And they went back and told the rest,
but they did not believe them.
Later he appeared to the eleven themselves
as they were sitting at the table;
and he upbraided them for their lack of faith
and stubbornness,
because they had not believed those who saw him
after he had risen.

—MARK 16:9–14

What did it take to convince you that the resurrection is true? Was it the reliability of the person or persons who taught you the story? Were they someone you trusted, and you believed because they believed? Sometimes, we just grow into our beliefs: you learn it as a child, you trust it in your youth, and you accept it as an adult. Other times, our beliefs come to us based on the influence someone might have in your world.

There's a story of how, one time, when the pope was visiting New York City, he had an appointment across town and was barely going to arrive at the scheduled time. The limo driver was doing fine until there was a breakdown in traffic. The pope got frustrated and insisted on driving the car. He was speeding along fast and recklessly, when he suddenly noticed a police car, siren and lights on, pulling up behind him. He pulled over and waited for the officer to come to his window. The officer asked why he was driving so fast. The pope explained, "We have an appointment on the other side of town and we're running late." The officer, a former altar boy, was shocked when he realized what was happening. He immediately called headquarters on his radio and requested a special police escort. When asked why and who it was for, he said, "I'm not sure, but the pope's driving him!" The pope had enough influence in the officer's life to make him believe something special about who might be riding in the back of the limo!

But our beliefs need not be based solely on whomever it is that teaches them. They need not be based on accepting the reliability of the stories that evoke them. We believe them because they are true. Still, whatever it was that convinced you, be thankful for that. And now, for those who do not believe … well, neither did the closest disciples of Jesus either. "When they heard that Jesus was alive and that she had seen Him, they did not believe it!" (Mark 16:11). They were still grieving deeply: "mourning and weeping" (v. 10). Perhaps it was hard to believe because, for them, it was just too good to be true. Perhaps they doubted the integrity of Mary Magdalene. After all she had been demon-possessed before Christ came into her life. And yet, the fact that Jesus had driven out seven demons from her life should give her something that few others had. She was blessed because she was free from such evil. I would give her credence!

And if Mary Magdalene's testimony to the risen Lord was not enough, well, here are two good men who had encountered Jesus resurrected out on a country road. When they reported having seen the Lord alive, "they did not believe them either!" (v. 13).

So, apart from Jesus coming personally to us, what would it take? I think we need to regain a sort of naïve trust like we might have had when we were children. By naïve, I don't mean ignorant or absent from reason. But the sort of trust that can depend on what someone trustworthy tells us. The way a child believes a parent.

I think we need to try this belief and see what it might do for us, the way we might be willing to try a drug to see if it heals us. Jesus prayed in the Garden of Gethsemane "for those who will believe in Me through their message … that all of them may be one" (John 17:20–21). That's you and me. We believe because we received their message from someone who received their message from someone who received their message, and so on. The climax to the Gospel of John comes when the risen Jesus says to Thomas, after he has been convinced, "Have you believed because you have seen me? Blessed are those who have not seen and yet believe!" (John 20:29). Peter repeats this in a very similar way. "Although you have not seen Him, you love Him; and even though you do not see Him now, you believe in Him and rejoice with indescribable and glorious joy" (1 Peter 1:8).

In Mark's story, when Jesus finally appears to the eleven, "He rebuked them for their lack of faith and their stubborn refusal to believe those who had seen Him after He had risen" (16:14). That stubborn refusal implies that the stories are false, and, therefore, those who said they'd seen Jesus alive after His resurrection are liars. If they are not liars, then, the death of Jesus must have been a hoax of some kind, and so we who believe today are fools!

Listen to what Paul says in 1 Corinthians 15: 13–17, 19:

> If Christ has not been raised, then our proclamation has been in vain and your faith has been in vain. We are even found to be misrepresenting God, because we testified of God that He raised Christ—whom He did not raise if it is true that the dead are not raised. For if the dead are not raised, then Christ has not been raised. If Christ has not been raised, your faith is futile and you are still in your sins … If for this life only we have hoped in Christ, we are of all people most to be pitied!

Paul implies that we don't need a savior if all we can hope for is confined to our mortal existence. But there is a kingdom that Jesus proclaimed, an eternal life that Jesus promised, and a glory that is yet to come!

Our belief gives us an assurance of these things. We believe in the resurrection because we experience the presence of Christ by faith. John wrote: "By this we know that Christ abides in us, by the Spirit that He has given us" (1 John 3:24b). There is an inward witness that comes by faith. Perhaps, not immediately, but we receive a sense that the truth is true, that the resurrection is real. If we do not have the Spirit of Christ, then what do we have? Is it just wishful thinking? Nearly two thousand years of wishful thinking? Or is the testimony of so many people of faith down through the generations a reliable witness? Can't we believe because so many others have been convinced?

You see, there is a power so palpable, an inspiration so pure, an assurance so powerful that we do not hesitate to accept the truth. It becomes a stubborn belief—a belief so strong that it fills us with hope, it lifts us up, it raises us to new life and to the glory of God. It is like a taste of heaven for us, a sense that the kingdom of God, where Jesus is King, has captured our hearts and minds and moves us to do on earth what Jesus did before us, and can now do within us and through us by His Holy Spirit.

So, we believe!

And the risen Christ told the eleven, "Go into all the world and preach the good news to all creation. Whoever believes and is Baptized will be saved, but whoever does not believe … will be condemned!" (Mark 16:15–16). Ahhh … the good news has some pretty bad news there. It's that old stubborn refusal comes to haunt us. It's out there, my friends. It breaks my heart because a lot of people we care about will be condemned because they don't believe! That alone should motivate us that we have a lot of convincing left to do!

PART 4
The Resurrection
in Luke

Some of the details in Luke are quite obviously different from the Gospel of Matthew. There is no earthquake at the moment of the resurrection in Luke. There are *two* angels who appear to more than two women. Their report to the disciples is not taken seriously at first. The angels ask the question, "Why do you look for the living among the dead?" (Luke 24:5). I love the story about the walk to Emmaus (vv. 13–32). There is no story about a Passover plot in Luke. And Jesus doesn't appear to the disciples until they meet him in Galilee, where Jesus reportedly (by Luke and Mark) told them to go. In Matthew, they were supposed to stay in Jerusalem.

These differences call us to try to account for whatever "problems" people might have with the text. I don't worry about it. Rarely do two or three witnesses agree completely when they testify. Different artists may stand in different places as they produce their paintings of the same setting. One will focus on different details than the others. Simply enjoy the gallery.

I will occasionally point out the differences, simply because it seems relevant to acknowledge them. I have watched several movies about World War II. They all have different foci, but it is the same war. There are the same battles; the perspectives of the directors may be very different, but the outcome is ultimately the same. There is a victory, there is surrender, and there is a liberation.

Look at the stories of the resurrection and just celebrate the ways they inspire you. Let's not overanalyze here. Meanwhile …

Wait till we study the resurrection in John!

Gone

But on the first day of the week, at early dawn,
they came to the tomb,
taking the spices that they had prepared.
They found the stone rolled away from the tomb,
but when they went in,
they did not find the body.
While they were perplexed about this,
suddenly two men in dazzling clothes stood beside them.
The women were terrified and bowed their faces to the ground,
but the men said to them,
"Why do you look for the living among the dead?
He is not here, but has risen.
Remember how he told you, while he was still in Galilee,
that the Son of Man must be handed over to sinners,
and be crucified,
and on the third day rise again."
Then they remembered his words,
and returning from the tomb,
they told all this to the eleven and to all the rest.
Now it was Mary Magdalene, Joanna, Mary the mother of James,
and the other women with them
who told this to the apostles.
But these words seemed to them an idle tale,
and they did not believe them.
But Peter got up and ran to the tomb,
stooping and looking in, he saw the linen cloths by themselves;
then he went home, amazed at what had happened.

—LUKE 24:1–12

Christian faith is so much more than a reaction to the absence of the dead body of Jesus. It is, however, in some respects, a reaction to the fact that, when they came to the tomb to anoint His body, He was gone! This is the launching point into the powerful mystery of the resurrection! He was gone! No matter how hard people have worked in their meager efforts to explain the empty tomb, Christianity has never really been able to be watered down by a supposed logic that would tell us that the idea of a resurrection is nonsense, an idle tale. Jesus was gone! They did not find the body!

On the first day of the week, that's Sunday, at early dawn, they came to the tomb; Jesus died on Friday. That's the first day. Sunset Friday was the beginning of the second day, as the Jews began the measure of their new day at the setting of the sun. And sunset Saturday evening began the third day. It was on the third day that Jesus rose from death. He had said it would be on the third day back in chapter 9 (v. 22), though the parallel to that passage in Mark 8 (v. 31) says, *after* three days. The fact that Jesus told His disciples ahead of time is a good indicator that He knew and trusted God's plan. "Remember," the angels said, "how He told you while He was still in Galilee, that the Son of Man must be handed over to sinners, and be crucified, and on the third day rise again!?" These two angels sure remembered!

They came to the tomb. Their intention was not to embalm, but to anoint the body of Jesus with spices, as well as ointments. The Jews did not embalm. What they did would help to mask the scent of death a bit, for a while, anyway. We all want death to be tolerable somehow. We don't know who they were who came to the tomb to anoint the body until verse 10 where it says it was Mary Magdalene, Joanna, Mary the mother of James, *and* the other women. It was a beautiful act of devotion they wanted to perform. They didn't have the time to do this on Friday before sunset. And sunset Friday to sunset Saturday was the Passover holy day. They couldn't do any work on a holy day, or a Sabbath. And because they needed daylight to see well enough to perform this ritual, they couldn't come until the sun rose again. So here they are.

In Luke, the stone that had been rolled against the opening of the tomb is more than just an obstacle. This was done with tombs like this to safeguard the deceased from any who might defile the body. But that stone likewise represented a sort of finality to the living. There is a barrier between the living and the dead that, generally, cannot be broken. I say generally because it seems there are occasional exceptions to this, as many living people have experienced the mystery of their loved one's presence after they have passed away. But the fact of the matter is that, in a very real way, they are gone. But on this exceptional occasion, "They found the stone rolled away from the tomb" (Luke 24:2). For Jesus, this barrier had been overcome somehow. Only in Matthew is there an explanation for how this was done: "Suddenly there was a great earthquake; for an angel of the Lord descending from heaven, came and rolled back the stone!" (Matthew 28:2). In the other Gospels, the way the story is told, the opening of the tomb is left a mystery.

They went in. Though the story does not mention it, I imagine a confused but curious pause among the women before they step through the opening of the tomb. Did they hesitate, thinking that, perhaps, someone else might have gotten there ahead of them? Putting ourselves in their place, we can all imagine what they might have been thinking. Their steps forward were probably filled with a combination of curiosity, purpose, and faith, and maybe fear.

"But when they went in, they did not find the body!" (24:3). Jesus was gone! Jesus was gone. Jesus was *gone*! Now what? "While they were perplexed about this, suddenly two men in dazzling white clothes stood beside them!" (vv. 3–4). Now most of us react a certain way when someone is *suddenly* standing beside us. At a minimum, we might be surprised. Most of us might feel a shock. In Mark, the women are "alarmed" (16:5). These women, it says in Luke, were "terrified!" (v. 5). The dazzling clothes tells you these were no ordinary men. The women felt a sense of reverence, and they "bowed their faces to the ground!" (v. 5b). They knew that something incredible had happened—or was happening!

The men said, "Why do you look for the living among the dead?" This question is asked only here, in the Gospel of Luke! In a way, the question makes very practical sense. What people are looking for when they visit a cemetery, however, is solace. Sometimes, it's resolution. Sometimes, it's about showing honor and respect for the memory of the one who is buried there. But an inner dialogue seems to continue between us and the person we've lost. It does not end at death. And though that dialogue is very one-sided after they're gone, we sometimes imagine what they might say if they were still here. What we might seek in a cemetery is meaning. The meaning of someone's life does not end when he or she dies. And though the meaning of that life is not found at the grave, that place can become an inspiration. It becomes a place that, like many other places, brings back his or her memory in very special ways! He is not here! After their question, the angels said, "He is not here!" Jesus was gone! Where?

Only in the Gospel of Matthew are we told they posted a guard and sealed the tomb so that the disciples couldn't steal the body of Christ and claim He had risen! But He *had* risen! He was *gone*. And the only thing that could ever prove without a doubt that Jesus had not risen would be for someone to have produced His dead body. And despite the vain efforts of human logic to explain away the resurrection, nothing can explain away the glorious power a belief in the resurrection of Christ has had on His followers! But either we believe in a lie, or we believe in the truth. If it was a lie, the Christian religion would have fizzled out centuries ago. And just the fact that we are here today tells the world that the resurrection of Christ means something greater than could ever be imagined. Without the resurrection, Christianity would be little more than a moral code, little more than a system of ethics, and little more than a series of wonderful stories. But because of the resurrection, we know that Jesus is who He claimed to be. Because of the resurrection, there is a wonderful source of wonder and mystery for us to ponder. Because of the resurrection, there is a religion, there is worship, there is belief, and there is hope!

If there is no resurrection of the dead, then Christ has not been raised; and if Christ has not been raised, then our proclamation has been in vain, and your faith is in vain. We are even found to be misrepresenting God, because we testified of God that He raised Christ—whom He did not raise if it is true that the dead are not raised. For if the dead are not raised, then Christ has not been raised. If Christ has not been raised, your faith is futile, and you are still in your sins. Then those also who have died in Christ have perished. If for this life only we have hoped in Christ, we are of all people most to be pitied (1 Corinthians 15:13–19).

The angels then reminded the women of the divine plan Christ had shared when He was alive. And then they remembered. And then they returned from the tomb! They did not return to business as usual. They did not return simply dazed by some vague confusion. They returned to the other disciples, and they told all this to the eleven and to the rest! They were not silent! They told. They told them that the stone had been moved! They told them that the tomb was opened! They told them that they went inside! They told them Jesus was gone! And they told them they'd seen angels! Angels that told them that Christ is risen!

But these words seemed to them an idle tale! And they did not believe them! (v. 11). It was too fantastic. It seemed too good to be true! I wonder if Lazarus was there. He had been dead, and Jesus raised *him* back to life! He probably wasn't, otherwise he would have said, "Yes!"

Yes! Something in the words of these women was sincere enough to make at least one of the disciples feel like he at least needed to see it for himself! It was Peter! He got up and ran to the tomb. In Luke, no one goes with him. He stooped and looked in, which tells you something about the dimensions of the opening to this tomb, and he saw the linen cloths Jesus had been covered with, but … no body! (v. 12). And then it says he went home. But like a pot of water over a fire, something was still happening within him. It says he was *amazed* at what had happened! (v. 12b). Amazed! It doesn't say he understood. It doesn't even say he believed. Most people would scoff at something they felt was unbelievable to them. So, I believe he believed. At least what was about to bubble up in him was belief. I think many Christians have a belief that's like that. Something amazes them about the power of faith, and, in a way, over time, they've gotten warmer; but there aren't any bubbles yet. There's a hope without commitment. There's a trust without confidence. There's acceptance without conviction. And there's heat but no fire. This is not true Christianity! It is the embryo of faith.

Come on! Christ is risen! He is risen indeed!

Come now. Let's fan those embers into flame!

The resurrection of Christ is not an idle tale to be told to the naive the way we tell the young about Santa Claus or the Easter Bunny. It is a fact. It is what proves to us that Jesus is who the scriptures say He is. It is what gives us pause to consider what Christ has done. The resurrection proves that Jesus is the Christ, and, that His suffering and death are exactly what God's Word says they are—they are our forgiveness. And nothing gives new life like knowing you're forgiven. Pay attention to the story of the prodigal son! New life! But we have more than new life. The power of the resurrection is what gives us eternal life! Come on! Christ is risen! He is risen indeed!

And in us who believe, there is a power that compels us to want others to know this hope that we have. The resurrection of Christ gives us hope for ourselves, hope for others, and hope for the world! The resurrection of Christ is what gives us a certainty about life beyond the grave, about the kingdom of heaven, and about those who are gone, and, that we'll meet them some day, when we all get to heaven.

The resurrection gives us something to live for. And it gives us a certainty that there is truly something to die for! Come on! Christ is risen! He is risen indeed! Yes!

To the Tomb and Back

They found the stone rolled away from the tomb,
but when they went in, they did not find the body.
While they were perplexed about this,
suddenly two men in dazzling clothes stood beside them.
The women were terrified and bowed their faces to the ground,
but the men said to them,
"Why do you look for the living among the dead?
He is not here, but has risen.

—LUKE 24:1–12

The journey to the tomb and back is not a long one, distance-wise. But it is like two different worlds. On the way to the tomb there was an incredible heaviness weighing on the hearts of the two Marys and Joanna, and the other women. On the way to the tomb, they carried spices to anoint the body of Jesus. On the way to the tomb there were tears in their eyes and sadness in their words. We know from the Gospel of Mark that they wondered how the stone at the entrance to the tomb would be removed. But they went anyway. They did so for themselves, as well as for Jesus. They were following protocol, but they had to come. It would hurt, but it would help.

The journey to the tomb reflects the human journey toward understanding and wisdom. In the not-knowing of the truth there is often a sense of feeling as though something is missing. It's not always an emptiness. It's more like a feeling of incompleteness. And so, we become seekers. If the women on the way to the tomb were seeking anything, though, it was more of a sense of doing themselves a favor by honoring their Lord. It was the least they could do now that He was dead. And it was the best they had to offer at the time.

Their journey turned into confusion, though. The stone was already out of their way! They looked inside the tomb, but Jesus was not there!

At first, they were perplexed. When you don't find what you expect to find where you expect to find it, you become filled with a mixture of disappointment and doubt, frustration and regret. You came all this way, and you didn't get what you wanted to get. You didn't get to do what you wanted to do. This is the dilemma for those who might come to church for answers, and all they seem to get is more questions. But then there comes a point in life where you realize that the journey is just as important as the destination, The process of seeking is just as powerful as what we hope to find. And we should never give up on our journeys because we might be exactly what someone else needed to find.

Well, their confusion didn't last very long. It turned into terror! Suddenly, two men in dazzling clothes were standing right beside them! (24:2). This was not sci-fi terror, where you are overwhelmed by evil. This was holy terror, awe before the power of the divine! They bowed their faces to the ground! (v. 5). Not because it was too much for them but because they felt so unworthy in the presence of angels. Their journey led them to this humble act of reverence. Could you still be reverent even though you didn't find what you were looking for, but you still found something?

The angels then asked one of the dumbest questions ever asked: "Why do you look for the living among the dead?" (v. 5b). It's a dumb question because they were not looking for a living person. They expected to find a dead body. And yet, in some ways, that's not that dumb a question. What was living at the tomb was their memory. Though the object of their affections was gone, they still felt their love for Jesus in their hearts. That was why they had come. And maybe that question becomes relevant when we realize that it could be asked in other ways, like: "Why are you living in the past when the future could be glorious?" Or, "Why do you want to go where you've already been, and do what you've already done while there are wonderful opportunities to explore all around you?" And the answer is in our comfort with what's familiar. We don't have to change our expectations. Well, the confusion returned. But it was a new confusion. It was a confusion filled with light because then, the angels gave the rationale for their question: "He is not here. He has risen!" (v. 5c). Jesus was alive? … a living person! Not a dead body! They began to understand.

But it wasn't easy. "Remember how he told you while He was still in Galilee …" (v. 6). That's the past. That seemed so long ago. That part of the journey seems far away. They're in Jerusalem now. But the past still matters. All we can remember is the past. You can't quite remember the future, can you. But the angels told them that, back in Galilee, Jesus had said, "the Son of Man must be handed over to sinners, and be crucified, and then rise again on the third day!" (v. 7).

And the light went on! "They remembered His words!" (v. 8).

And the journey back from the tomb began. Their sadness had become joy; their purpose had gone from anointing a dead man to proclaiming a new life. The power of the cross receives its anointing through the miracle of the resurrection. The death of Jesus that takes away the sin of the world is proven by the rising of Jesus to take His throne in His heavenly kingdom!

And we, even today, can only begin to understand. The journey back to the others could be happy now because even though they might not have found what they were looking for, they were still filled with joy. And in our journeys, we may not find what we expect to find, but, like those women, we still have something to say. And even though the others may not believe what we have to say, we need to trust that hopefully, someday, the understanding will come.

You see, the world, and those belonging to the world, don't want to hear what we've got to say. At least, not at first. They can't bear the message of the resurrection. To the world, it is just an "idle tale." But are they liars? The Gospel writers? The apostles? Paul said in 1 Corinthians 15:14–15: "If Christ has not been raised, then our proclamation has been in vain and your faith has been in vain! We are even found to be misrepresenting God!"

The resurrection is either true, or it is not true. However it may be watered down or doctored up, the world has to face the fact that the church is real. We are real. We are not just an idle tale!

"Peter got up and ran to the tomb; stooping and looking in, he saw the linen cloths by themselves. Then … he went home! … amazed!" (v. 12).

Rediscover for your life that amazement. Everyone in every church in every land should have that same amazement that Peter had. The world will look at us and maybe … maybe at least some will join that journey, the journey that leads to the tomb and back. And maybe … maybe they'll discover what we have come to understand: That Jesus died for our sin … Amazing grace! … but that He rose to give us new life! Amazing life!

They Did Not Believe Them

Now it was Mary Magdalene, Joanna,
Mary the mother of James,
and the other women with them.

—LUKE 24:10

The first day: It was the first day of the week. God began creating on that day! (Genesis 1:5).

Early dawn: Still mostly dark, but you can see. It's not daylight, but it's not night. It's like a state of numbness, as if existence were dangling above a flowing stream, just about to enter the water. Inert, but about to come alive. It's like a time of being mostly confident and somewhat uncertain at the same time. Perhaps most of us have lived through such a state. Nothing is happening, but something's about to happen. Something has ended, but something's about to begin. It's like the silence before the next song begins.

They came: The storyteller uses the special effect of anonymity at first. *They* came. We don't know who *they* are (yet), but they came to the tomb of Jesus. They had a purpose. A purpose that seemed well correlated to that unreal time of day. They had with them the spices that they had prepared. Prepared for the body of Jesus. They came to offer Him this final honor. To anoint His body with ointment to cleanse its skin. To sprinkle spices, some that would absorb the odor of decay, some that would give the tomb a tolerable scent, and some that would prevent animals and flies (mostly flies) from preying on the flesh. It was at once a beautiful thing they wanted (had) to do and an awkward but necessary task for a respected person whose life had ended.

The stone: At the opening to the tomb, a large stone had been placed. Some say that the stone had been sealed the day after Jesus was buried (Matthew 27:66). This was supposed to secure the grave from being broken into by Jesus's disciples who, they thought, might steal His body to fake a resurrection. Even guards were posted ... *on the second day.* Luke, however, tells of no guards, no earthquakes, no divine intervention to roll away the stone. But the stone ... it had been rolled away! They *found* it that way! And they went into the tomb ... and they did not find the body!

Perplexed: The Greek word is *diaporea*—"out of sorts." They were perplexed. That early dawn feeling tightened. What now? This makes no sense! They stood still, but inwardly they were staggering. Bewildered by the unexpected but sure about ... something! They looked into each other's faces ... for an answer? No. For reassurance. Without making a sound, the look in their eyes asked the same question: What could this mean? It was like a pause—to ponder the significance of that moment—was welling up in the space that encircled them, but it was silent, a silence that was ready to burst. It was silent. Silent.

Suddenly: Two men in dazzling clothes stood beside them! The air was now filled with the sound of gasps. By now, the dawning of the day was such that sight was easy; light was present, though the sun was not. Shouldn't they have seen these two coming? How could they be missed? These two were not ordinary people!

Terrified: The women were terrified! Not because they were surprised or shocked (though they were) but because they knew that these men in dazzling clothes must be messengers of God. Angels! The Hebrew word for messenger of God is *angel*! Terror filled them. Not a terror from feeling threatened but a terror of awe, of reverence, of fear as when in the presence of something holy. And so, they bowed. Afraid to look directly at these two men in dazzling clothes, they bowed their faces to the ground.

The men said: These two men spoke! Words they could understand. All they could do was listen ... and tremble. "Why do you look for the living among the dead?" They weren't! They were looking for Jesus. Jesus was dead! "He is not here!" This they now knew. Remember, they were perplexed when they did not find His body! "He has risen!" They might have been there when Jesus brought the widow's son back to life in Nain. And then there was Jairus's daughter. If they weren't there, surely they would have heard about His miracles from someone who was.

Remember: "Remember how He told you, while He was still in Galilee, that the Son of Man must be handed over to sinners, and be crucified, and on the third day rise again!" Remember! Their minds were racing with so many memories.

They remembered: They remembered His words. The expression on each of their faces became one of recognition. Something special was welling up in their hearts. It was not joy, not yet, anyway. It was excitement. Joy was right around the corner, and they knew it. But the way Luke tells the story, they were restrained. As they remembered that Jesus had said He would rise, they forgot all about the two men in dazzling clothes. Were they still there? Were they basking in the blessing of seeing their hearers' faces light up? Like parents on the morning of their toddler's birthday, they knew what was in store, but it was still the not-yet time before the reason for the excitement finally arrives.

Did they disappear? Angels seem to disappear once they've given their message. At His birth, the whole heavenly host sang. *"Glory to God in the highest!"* One second they were there; the next, they were gone. The storyteller never mentions the two men again.

They told: Returning from the tomb … Did they just w*alk* back? The storyteller simply says, returning from the tomb. Their approach at early dawn was dark, dry, muted, sad. But now the atmosphere would have been electric. They were changed. Renewed! Reborn! Excitement made their hearts pound. I would think they at least hurried! Eagerness set them on fire! Returning from the tomb, they told all this to the eleven (Judas was not with them anymore) and to all the rest! They had a message! They could tell everyone that they had heard the voices of angels! He is not here. He has risen! What a wonderful message! What a glorious truth! What perfect news they had to share.

Now: Who were they? It was Mary Magdalene, Joanna, Mary the mother of James and the other women with them who told this to the apostles! At least five women! Mark tells us it was Mary Magdalene, Mary the mother of James, and Salome (16:1). Matthew tells us it was Mary Magdalene and the other Mary! (28:1). John tells us it was only Mary Magdalene! (20:1). However the story is told, women were the first to hear the glorious news! Women were the first to share it! What did the men do?

An idle tale: The words of these women seemed to them to be an idle tale, and they did not believe them. It was more than doubt. It was just too amazing to be true. But the women had seen the tomb—empty. They had heard what *angels* had said—He is not here. He has risen! They shared the wonderful experience they had had only moments ago. It set their hearts on fire! They did not believe them. Did they think the women were liars? No. They just couldn't believe it was real. It was an idle tale, a myth, a story, like something a child might tell other children boastfully. Surely, they exaggerated. This was too fabulous. They did not believe them.

The women must have suddenly felt so unappreciated, so taken for granted, so insignificant. The condescending attitude of the apostles was downright offensive. Here they were on fire, and nobody's catching the heat! The apostles were unimpressed. But all of us resist the spectacular during the familiar. We would shrug off the glory that comes to those too close to us that we would feel embarrassed by their exuberance. They did not believe them. Their doubt could not discredit the women. They must have held fast to their story. Jesus had suffered so much only days before. He had died on a cross—an innocent man, a wonderful teacher, a humble messiah. But *was* He the Messiah? This was the question clouding their minds. *Was* He alive again? How was it possible? For the women, it was indisputable. Nothing could challenge what they knew in their hearts. But this was just too good to be true. This was beyond belief. They did not believe them.

Peter: Peter got up. He couldn't contain himself. They insisted. He resisted. But, you know, nothing quite works on you like a heart on fire! Peter ran to the tomb. He must have known where it was, though only some of the women saw where Jesus's body had been laid. But … he ran. Did others go with him? They must have. How else could this story be told unless Peter told it himself. He stooped. The size of the opening was small, or it opened downward, or his body blocked the daylight. Stooping at the opening, he looked in. All he saw were the linen cloths—by themselves. No body. No clues. No angels. No men in dazzling clothes.

He went home: Stunned. Numb. All the storyteller says is that he went home. Where else could he go? He probably walked slowly in stunned silence. But he was amazed. Surprised. But curious. He marveled at what had happened.

Jesus had risen!

Nothing could ever be the same. As the facts sank in, he surely knew it was true. Now, he must turn the disbelief of the others into understanding.

Jesus overcame death. God had raised Him from His grave! Death was defeated. Faith had its victory. Peter had to absorb it all. They did not believe. But what could convince them?

They did not believe, at first. Soon they would be so convinced that they began to set the whole world on fire!

Are you convinced? The fire's still burning? What more do you need?

Christ is risen! He is risen … indeed!

Remember

"Why do you look for the living among the dead?
He is not here, but has risen. Remember how he told you,
while he was still in Galilee,
that the Son of Man must be handed over to sinners,
and be crucified,
and on the third day rise again."
Then they remembered his words.

—LUKE 24:5B-8

W hen it seems impossible to see the way forward, look back. Remember. Remember what Jesus said. Go back to a point of reference. Go back to that time when Jesus had been praying with His disciples, and He interrupted His prayers and asked, the question: "Who do the crowds say that I am?" (Luke 9:18). Remember their answers: "John the Baptist, Elijah, one of the ancient prophets has arisen!" (Luke 9:19). Elijah had been taken up into heaven by a divine chariot. He had never really died. It was thought that this greatest of prophets would return some day. There was also the curious idea held by a few small handfuls of the people of Israel that a great prophet of the past, even though they had all died (except Elijah), might arise. All three possibilities—John the Baptist, Elijah, and the prophets—were messianic hopefuls in the minds of most Israelites. "But who do you say that I am?" Peter answered, "You are the Messiah of God!" (Luke 9:20).

Peter was plain and simple, insightful and honest, bold and aware. Jesus was the Messiah! But Jesus, back in chapter 9, ordered them not to make it known. He knew the understanding in that day of who the Messiah was supposed to be was not that of the redeemer, the Lamb of God who takes away the sin of the world. The common notion was that the Messiah would be a political/military leader who would deliver Israel from oppression. The idea had little to do with faith. Jesus said, "The Son of

Man must undergo great suffering, and be rejected by the Elders, the Chief Priests and the Scribes, and be killed, and … on the third day be raised!" (v. 22). And this is exactly what these two angels told Mary Magdalene, Joanna, Mary the mother of James, and the other women with them!

Remember … Remember how during His travels, on His way to Jerusalem for the last time, some Pharisees who were friendly to Jesus informed Him that Herod was out to get Him. "Go and tell that fox, 'Behold, I am casting out demons and performing cures today and tomorrow, and … on the third day … I finish my work! Yet today, tomorrow, and the next day I must be on my way, because it is impossible for a prophet to be killed outside Jerusalem!'" (13:32 33).

Remember. Jesus *had* spoken of His death, but He'd also said something about the third day! His work was not finished at the cross. His death did not complete His purpose. It was His resurrection that was God's finishing touch. "Then they remembered His words!" The angels were plain and simple, insightful and honest, bold and aware.

"Why do you look for the living among the dead?" Why? Because we want to remember, The grave is a point of reference. Even after we've said our last goodbyes, there is something that draws us back to that place to say farewell again. But we do not say it to the one in the grave; we say it to something within that is gone.

The women were not looking for someone living. They wanted to anoint the body of Jesus, who died, who was buried there. They were not doing something out of the ordinary. They were doing something very honorable. But "they did not find the body!" The tomb was empty! The stone had been rolled away! Luke does not explain how, only Matthew does. Who? How? "They were perplexed about this!"

The resurrection is perplexing! Paul spoke about it:

"Now if Christ is preached as raised from the dead, how can some of you say that there is no resurrection of the dead? But if there is no resurrection of the dead, then Christ has not been raised; if Christ has not been raised, then our preaching is in vain and your faith is in vain. We are even found to be misrepresenting God, because we testified of God that He raised Christ, whom He did not raise if it is true that the dead are not raised. For if the dead are not raised, then Christ has not been raised. If Christ has not been raised, your faith is futile and you are still in your sins.

Then those who have fallen asleep in Christ have perished. If for this life only we have hoped in Christ, we are of all people most to be pitied. But, in fact, Christ *has* been raised from the dead!" (1 Corinthians 15:12–20a).

Are we "misrepresenting God because we testify of God that He raised Christ?" (1 Corinthians 15:15). Did the women lie? Did the disciples lie? Did the Gospel writers lie? Have church leaders down through the ages perpetuated a lie? "But when they went in, they did not find the body!" Only the dead body of Jesus could ever absolutely prove there had been no resurrection. "He is not here," the angels said, "but has risen!" Remember, the resurrection of Christ is not just theology!

"Then they remembered His words, and returning from the tomb, they told all this to the Eleven and to all the rest … But these words seemed to them an idle tale, and they did not believe" (Luke 24:8–10). The Greeks and Romans had mythological tales that no one really believed. They were mostly entertaining, even though they still gave homage to their false gods. That Christ had risen was just too good to believe, too impossible to accept, too miraculous to understand, too mythical to trust.

But the resurrection proves that Jesus is the Messiah, the One who died for our sins. Jesus took upon Himself all the guilt of all the sin of all the world even though He was completely innocent. He was holy. And the resurrection proves His innocence. Jesus was holy, and nothing holy, divine, perfect, can ever be separated from God, can ever know the corruption of death, can ever end!

This was the understanding of that day, and we need to remember it. The apostles said nothing at first. Their minds were digesting what the women had said. Slowly, perhaps, it began to sink in. I picture Peter rubbing his beard, scratching his head, thinking it over, remembering, remembering … remembering. Finally, "Peter got up and ran to the tomb" (v. 12). Maybe this was not an idle tale. Maybe Jesus did rise. Maybe death could not hold Him. Maybe the power of God is greater than we can imagine. "Stooping and looking in, he saw the linen cloths by themselves!" (v. 12b). Something awesome had obviously taken place. Peter's heart was pounding. He could feel every beat throbbing in his chest. His blood pulsed in his veins. The tomb did not have a body!

He caught his breath. He kept looking but didn't see Jesus. "Then he went home" (v. 12c) Where else do you go? Nothing could ever be the same again. He would have to change his way of thinking—about everything! His mind raced from what before had been defeat to what now was a sense of victory. Though it was tenuous at first, it was still victory. How do you absorb the most powerful occurrence the world had ever known? Peter didn't just go home, though. It says, "he went home, amazed at what had happened" (v. 12c-d).

Even though he might not have been sure if he believed it all yet, at least he was amazed. At a minimum, this should be our posture before just the suggestion of this impossible miraculous reality. Just be amazed. The women did not lie. Peter did not lie. The Gospel writers did not lie. The Christian leaders of the past twenty centuries did not lie. Believe it; it is plain and simple, insightful and honest, bold and aware. Christ is risen. It's amazing!

Stay

_____

Now on that same day
two of them were going to the village of Emmaus,
about seven miles from Jerusalem,
and talking with each other about all these things that had happened.
While they were talking and discussing,
Jesus himself came near and went with them,
but their eyes were kept from recognizing him.
And he said to them,
"What are you discussing with each other while you walk along?"
They stood still, looking sad.
Then one of them, whose name was Cleopas, answered him,
"Are you the only stranger in Jerusalem
who does not know the things that have taken place there in these days?"
He asked them, "What things?"
They replied, "The things about Jesus of Nazareth,
who was a prophet mighty in deed and word before God and all the people,
and how our chief priests and leaders handed him over
to be condemned to death and crucified him.
But we had hoped that he was the one to redeem Israel.
Yes, and besides all this,
it is now the third day since these things had taken place.
Moreover, some women of our group astounded us.
They were at the tomb early this morning,
and when they did not find the body there,
they came back
and told us that they had indeed seen a vision of angels
who said he was alive.
Some of those who were with us went to the tomb
and found it just as the women had said;
but they did not see him."
Then he said to them,
"Oh how foolish you are, and how slow of heart to believe
all that the prophets have declared.
Was it not necessary that the Messiah should suffer these things

and then enter into his glory?"
Then beginning with Moses and all the prophets,
he interpreted to them the things about himself in all the scriptures.
As they came near the village to which they were going,
he walked ahead as if he were going on.
But they urged him strongly, saying,
"Stay with us,
because it is almost evening and the day is nearly over."
So he went to stay with them.
When he was at the table with them,
he took bread, blessed and broke it, and gave it to them.
Then their eyes were opened and they recognized him;
and he vanished from their sight.
They said to each other,
"Were not our hearts burning within us
while he was talking to us on the road,
while he was opening the scriptures to us?"
That same hour they got up and returned to Jerusalem;
and they found the eleven and their companions, gathered together.
They were saying,
"The Lord has risen indeed, and he has appeared to Simon!"
Then they told what had happened on the road,
and how he had been made known to them in the breaking of the bread.

—LUKE 24:13–35

Archimedes said, "Give me a place to stand, and I can move the world!" Belief in Jesus is like having a place to stand, and the resurrection is the lever!

THAT SAME DAY

Two disciples, one named Cleopas, the other unknown, left the others behind in Jerusalem. Sometimes, you just need to get away, to go somewhere, anywhere but "here." Especially when you feel a mixture of confusion and grief. The city may have felt like it was closing in on them. The Passover crowds would have lingered for many days. Too many people. Too much noise. They needed some breathing room. A walk in the country may have seemed like just the right thing to do. Where do you go when you need to "get away?" Maybe Cleopas lived in Emmaus; maybe the unknown disciple lived there. The walk would do them good.

A VILLAGE NAMED EMMAUS

Emmaus is "Everytown." It is where "Anyone" lives. Many Romans, most of them soldiers, are thought to have lived there because, as some scholars believe, it was later established as a Roman colony. Either way, it doesn't really matter when you consider the road to Emmaus as the road on which is met the risen Christ. In that regard, we are all on "the road to Emmaus." We all meet Christ, either by searching for Him, or by chance. As often as not, Jesus is met while we are going somewhere. Where have you been going when you met the risen Christ? We can't help but encounter Him though. He was sent by God to the whole world. Everyone must face the reality of Jesus Christ at some time or other, whether that reality is only the idea of a risen savior or the power of Christ that overcomes death.

TALKING ABOUT ALL THE THINGS
THAT HAD HAPPENED

Jesus was so much on their minds that they couldn't help but talk about Him. There is a cathartic release that comes from talking things through when you've experienced the sort of shock those disciples were feeling. Recounting the events of the past three or four days would have been painful, but it would also have helped them sort out their feelings. If anything, they would have spoken about what Jesus meant to them personally, if not about what he may have meant, or now means to the whole world. They might have been telling each other what they thought it meant that they all felt as though the women's encounter with angels telling them that Jesus had risen was just "an idle tale" (Luke 24:11). Who do you talk to to sort out your feelings?

THEIR EYES WERE KEPT FROM
RECOGNIZING HIM

The only reason the risen Christ would have been walking the road alone would have been to encounter these two disciples. Somehow, Christ knew their need. He came to bring them understanding, to open their eyes, and their hearts. And through them, to open our eyes and our hearts. But their eyes were kept from recognizing Him at first. Something inhibited, not their sight, not their vision, but their perception. It's difficult, at first, sometimes, to see the blessing right before us until it truly overwhelms us! Like the fireworks rocket launched into the sky, it leaves a wonderful streak but has not yet burst into a thousand beautiful sparkles; we may feel something, but we really feel it when it explodes. These two disciples felt something when Christ joined them on the road, but they didn't yet understand it. Their pace may have been very slow, so they were easily overtaken by this "stranger." And He asked them what they'd been discussing.

A STILLNESS AND A SADNESS

The question stopped them in their tracks. For a moment they just stood still, looking sad. Perhaps that was the most natural response to the cheerful sort of "hello" they had been given. When the conversation is so deep and the grief and confusion so heavy, you can't help but pause a moment to shift gears to bring someone else up to speed. And so they gave the condensed version: "Concerning Jesus of Nazareth, who was a mighty prophet in deed and word before God and all the people, and how the Chief Priests and rulers delivered Him up to be condemned to death, and crucified Him" (Luke 24:19–20). Jesus could have stopped them any time. But perhaps it was good to let them share their perspective. That way, He would have been able to discern exactly where their anguish lay. And sometimes, there is an advantage in being able to talk about yourself as if you were not there and nobody knew you. And then they said, "But we had hoped that He was the one to redeem Israel!" (v. 21). There is a bit of disappointment there: "We *had* hoped." It implies, "But now we don't know what to think." That is the status of the human condition, especially now. Many people just don't know what to think. The world is not turning out the way they thought it should. They're confused. Faithful, but unsure. Believing but unable to invest complete trust without some absolutes.

SOME WOMEN AMAZED US

"What's more, this is the third day, and some women of our fellowship amazed us! They were at the tomb early this morning and did not find His body! And, they came back saying they had seen a vision of angels, who said He was alive!" (vv. 21b–23). They want to believe it, but the words "an idle tale" (24:11) kept rising in their minds. Something has happened, that's for sure. But they just didn't know what to think about it. Some of the other disciples checked their story. Yes, there was an empty tomb, but they saw no angels.

SLOW OF HEART TO BELIEVE

Wasn't it simpler, once, when as a child, in our innocence, we took people at their word? A story about angels didn't confuse us then; it fascinated us. It drew us in very compelling ways. Until someone, usually a few years older, with a bold tone of arrogance, would say, "Oh, that couldn't happen." Or, "Angels aren't real." Or, they would laugh and just say, "That's dumb." And ever since that moment, we began to believe more slowly, to doubt more immediately. Jesus even seems to take that arrogant tone, but with them, it is used in favor of belief and in censure of doubt. Then, "beginning with Moses and all the prophets, He interpreted to them all the scriptures concerning Himself!" (v. 27). Slowly, seriously, the two disciples began to be convinced. The way this stranger taught them drew them to Him. Like thirsty men after crossing a barren desert, they thirsted for more from Him.

STAY WITH US

They felt a connection so strong they felt as though they had gained a new friend. They offered Him their hospitality, and He accepted it. Perhaps they felt the way you feel when you are waking up in the middle of a beautiful dream. You don't want it to end. "Stay with us." Their hearts were burning within them, ignited by the truth of all they were hearing. "Stay with us." A hunger was being fed. A sweetness filled them. "Stay with us." Don't leave. We want you around, if just for a little while more. "Stay with us." Let us feed you! "Stay." Their appeal was from their burning hearts.

THEIR EYES WERE OPENED

When they were at table, He took the bread and blessed it. He broke it. And he held it out to them (v. 30). Suddenly, as they received it, their eyes were opened. I picture Jesus vanishing the moment He let go of the bread. In their moment of recognition, He no longer needed to stay. And His vanishing out of their sight sealed their belief. Their doubt vanished. Their confusion faded away. They understood now. I picture a smile on the face of Christ, and a twinkle in His eye, as they looked up from the bread they were receiving. They may have noticed the scars in His hands, and finally they took a serious look into the face of their companion. But even before they really looked, they knew. And as soon as they looked, there was nothing to see!

But now they had faith. And "faith is ... the conviction of things not seen" (Hebrews 11:1).

The first thing they said to each other was, "Didn't our hearts burn within us even back on the road, even as He opened to us the Scriptures?" (Luke 24:32).

As we celebrate the risen Christ, don't our hearts burn within us? As we sing about the glorious power of the faith known in the joy of Easter, don't our hearts resonate within? As we consider the resurrection of Christ, don't our hearts swell with gladness at the knowledge that even death has been conquered?

O hearts afire, stay with us!

O burning faith, stay with us! O glorious power, stay!

To Emmaus and Back

As they came near the village to which they were going,
he walked ahead as if he were going on.
But they urged him strongly, saying,
"Stay with us,
because it is almost evening and the day is nearly over."
So he went to stay with them.
When he was at the table with them,
he took bread, blessed and broke it, and gave it to them.
Then their eyes were opened and they recognized him;
and he vanished from their sight.
They said to each other,
"Were not our hearts burning within us
while he was talking to us on the road,
while he was opening the scriptures to us?"
That same hour they got up and returned to Jerusalem;
and they found the eleven and their companions, gathered together.
They were saying,
"The Lord has risen indeed, and he has appeared to Simon!"
Then they told what had happened on the road,
and how he had been made known to them in the breaking of the bread.

—LUKE 24:28–35

The journey to Emmaus from Jerusalem is a slow two-hour walk. It is a scenic walk, an easy walk, a pleasant walk. But that afternoon, it was a long, heavy walk. Or, at least, it started out that way. The journey to Emmaus is a journey of transformation. It is a process of change, of enlightenment, of eyes being opened. It is not an easy journey, but it is the sort of journey that you would be glad to take.

Two disciples of Jesus who couldn't sit still after all the things that had happened, were making their way to the home of Cleopas in a town about seven miles away. There was nothing they could gain by staying in Jerusalem. At least, I imagine that's what they might have thought.

From Friday evening till Sunday morning, the only thing they'd been thinking about and talking about was the Crucifixion and death of Jesus. Sometimes, the only way to feel as though you can begin to understand your grief is by talking about the circumstances that have caused it.

"Why did Jesus go to Gethsemane that night? He always went there. He should have gone to Bethany, and Lazarus could have hidden Him." "Why did the apostles run away?" "Why did Judas betray the Teacher?" "Did you hear about how Peter denied knowing Him?" Questions rise and speculative answers get tossed around. And through that process, at a minimum, you can at least get a grip on all that happened. It may not take the pain away, it may not bring clear answers, but it helps us understand.

As Jerusalem was returning to business as usual, for some, it was too difficult to just go forward. They needed time. They needed quiet. They needed to escape the activity and noise of the city. These two must have had to get away from it all, clear their heads, get a change of scenery, change the subject. But they couldn't escape the subject. There was a new twist to the story that had come up. The women who went to the tomb didn't find Jesus. Angels told them He was alive. Peter and John had gone to see. Jesus was gone. Their conversation now may have revolved around the idea of "What if Jesus *is* alive?" "How?" "How are the dead raised?"

Perhaps they drew up the story of Elijah and how he had raised the widow's son in Zarephath so long ago (1 Kings 17:17–23). That may have brought to mind the way Jesus had raised a man in the city of Nain, another widow's son (Luke 7:11–15). Is there some way Jesus had a power over death, a power of life? Could He have had a power over His own death?

Wherever their conversation led them, I want to believe there was a confused sort of hope that rose to the surface now and then. But amid it all, a stranger joined them. It was Jesus, but they didn't know it. Now back then, you didn't just join other travelers. As you came near, you would ask if you could join them first. And always, then, you were welcomed to do so. There might be introductions, or there might not. In this case, I guess there were not. You can imagine that Jesus spoke with a cheerful tone when He asked them, "What are you discussing as you walk along?" And rather than look at their new companion, they must have stopped and looked at one another, dumbfounded. They were downcast. Melancholy. Sad. And finally, one of them asked, "Are you the only stranger in Jerusalem who does not know the things that have taken place there?"

They must have still been relatively close to Jerusalem. The assumption seems to be that the stranger has just left the city as well. Still, He wanted to learn what they knew about what had been happening in Jerusalem. And now their transformation begins. They shared what they believed about Jesus. That "He was a prophet mighty in deed and in word!" That Jesus had been condemned and crucified. And that they believed He could have been the One to set Israel free. But now they're not so sure. They were obviously confused, especially by the report of how that morning He had risen … or had He?

Then the journey takes on a whole new tone. The stranger begins to explain how the Crucifixion, death, and resurrection were all prophesied in the scriptures. It must have all been part of a divine plan. And passage after passage, the stranger revealed the truth they needed to know. The journey is no longer heavy, but it is deep. It is no longer filled with the darkness of grief but with the light of life. In some respects, all of us take this journey. It is the journey through the valley of the shadow of death, but it is also a journey where we discover that there is no cause for fear, because God is with us. It is a journey that softens our grief by the knowledge that a new life has come for the one we have lost. It is a journey that not only transforms us but that alters our perspective on death.

And the two disciples urged the stranger, "Stay with us." Keep this light coming. Don't let it end. But there is an end of sorts. When their eyes were opened, the journey continues. But it is a journey back—back to Jerusalem. Back to the others. Others needed to know what they knew. The others needed to hear what they now understood.

The journey back to Jerusalem is not back to an old way. It is not back to business as usual. It is back to a new life. The transformation is not complete until it transforms others. They would be a new community! They would become Easter people! The followers of the risen Christ! They would become the church!

They Still Disbelieved ... For Joy

While they were talking about this,
Jesus himself stood among them
and said to them, "Peace be with you."
They were startled and terrified, and thought they were seeing a ghost.
He said to them, "Why are you frightened,
and why do doubts arise in your hearts?
Look at my hands and my feet; see that it is I myself.
Touch me and see;
for a ghost does not have flesh and bones as you see that I have."
And when he had said this, he showed them his hands and his feet.
While they were disbelieving and still wondering, he said to them,
"Have you anything here to eat?"
They gave him a piece of broiled fish,
and he took it and ate it in their presence.

—LUKE 24:36–43

How odd it must have felt to be told by a stranger that they were foolish and slow of heart. They had entrusted their souls to Jesus. But He'd been crucified. He was the Messiah, they thought, but so much was left unfinished. *"We had hoped that He was the one to redeem Israel!"* We *had* hoped! For very practical reasons, their hope had vanished. It might have felt like you'd feel when the team's best player is injured in practice just before the big game. They had depended on Jesus to be the one to make the difference they hoped for. It is not foolish to be confused when your dreams have been crushed—when the greatest thing that ever happened to you is killed. The chief priests and leaders of the Jews did not think that way. Maybe they were right all along!?

When defeat happens, it is only logical to retreat, to surrender to the reality that the one you thought could redeem Israel must not have been who they thought He was. Maybe all He'd really been was "a prophet mighty in deed and word before God and all the people" (Luke 24:19). Not too bad really. But they had wanted Jesus to be *the One!* Even more distressing is the confusion they couldn't shake because there were some women from among their group that had gone to the tomb that morning and didn't find the body of Jesus. Not only that, but … "They had seen a vision of angels who said He was alive!" (Luke 24:23). A few others had gone to see if it could be true, and, yes, the tomb was empty (24:12).

Confusion. That's where many people leave the resurrection of Jesus. And because it's too confusing, too incredible, they just shrug it off and say they don't believe. Confusion. Grieving over the loss on Friday; discouraged by the disappointment of a very long Saturday, and perplexed by the disappearance of the body that morning, their eyes were as downcast as their hearts. Squinting as they faced the setting sun, they barely looked at their new companion on the road to Emmaus who has told them, now, that they were foolish and slow of heart (24:25). And He explained to them all the reasons they had to believe that Jesus was *the One!* When you examine all the prophetic visions of what the Messiah was supposed to be and do, how could they not believe?

Fascinated by this stranger's interpretations, they compelled Him to stay with them. The sun had set by now. It was not dark yet but growing dim. The day was over. It was time to eat. So, He joined them as their guest. It was a simple meal. The stranger—how odd to have never even asked His name—said a prayer, and, when He broke the bread, they saw His hands. They had wounds as if He'd been crucified! A flash of recognition came to the two men. They looked at each other and knew exactly what the other was thinking. They probably wanted to fall at His feet, but when they turned back to where Jesus had been sitting, He was gone. Two pieces of broken bread were left on the table.

They didn't eat. They didn't say, "Hey! That stranger was Jesus!" They said something that reassured themselves. "Were not our hearts burning within us while He was talking to us on the road? While He was opening the Scriptures to us?" (24:32). During that hour on the road, there must have been many moments when they nodded about what the stranger was saying, thinking, "Yes! *That* was Jesus!" Understanding and inspiration, depth and meaning, and now, knowledge. Nothing is more convincing than experience!

They had to get back to Jerusalem. They had to tell the eleven. It wasn't theological insight they wanted to share; it was their experience. We may never, in our lifetimes, see Jesus, risen and triumphant. But there were those who did. And when we hear their story, do not our hearts burn within us? The road back from Emmaus must have felt electric now. That's where we are. We are with them, understanding and inspired, knowing that Jesus is risen! Risen indeed!

The apostles were still all gathered together when they finally joined them. Before they could get their news out, someone blurted out that "The Lord is risen indeed, and … He has appeared to Simon!" (24:34). Then, the eleven listened to their testimony, fascinated, hearts on fire! Then— *boom*! Jesus appeared to all of them! His first words were, "Peace be with you!" (24:36). Startled, terrified, not sure, confused—they thought they were seeing a ghost! Oh, how foolish! How slow of heart!

Jesus was really there! He showed them the wounds in His hands and His feet. It was Jesus! They still disbelieved. But this time … this time … it was because it just seemed too good to be true. It was not doubt. It was not confusion. They may have still felt a bit perplexed because they couldn't imagine *how* it could have happened, and that's another hang-up for many people. The how is not as important as the truth that it *did* happen in the first place. They were just overjoyed. And though we might not get that feeling today, since we've absorbed the reality with years of belief, trusting the testimony of centuries of others who found the heart-warming truth in death's defeat at Christ's victory, we can tell the story. We can share our experience of the resurrection power of faith we know when we trust in Jesus as our savior.

Their cups were running over. I imagine that they kept glancing back at their risen Savior, to be sure He was really there. I picture them as they keep pinching themselves to be sure they weren't just dreaming. And then, Jesus did something that brought them all down to earth, back to reality, and probably made them laugh out loud. He asked, "Got anything to eat?" (24:41). He wasn't hungry. He didn't need to eat. He had a glorified body. It could appear and disappear. He didn't need to eat, but He did, for their sake. It made Him just that much more real. And like the good Methodists that they were, whenever they gathered, they had food! Somebody passed the broiled fish, and He ate some! You can bet that made the cook happy. The risen Lord ate some of my specialty!

Is it too good to be true … today? Have we explained away the reality that Jesus rose from death and turned it into little more than theological ideas? Is it just an idea for you, or did Jesus truly rise? Does your heart burn within you? As the scriptural testimony is shared, does it inspire you? We need to realize that if we don't believe, or if we know someone who doesn't believe it, it's as good as saying that Luke was lying. It's as good as saying that I am a fool for believing his words. Centuries of believers have trusted the truth that Jesus Christ is risen! Why can't you?

Be convinced! It's a power that changes you. It's a glory that ignites a fire! Give it fuel! Let it burn! And go, convince the rest of the world!

The Entry into Glory

*"Was it not necessary
that the Messiah should suffer these things
and then enter into his glory?"*

—LUKE 24:26

Somewhere in time, there was a man who was lost. He didn't know how he became lost, he only knew that he was lost. Perhaps he had always been lost, it was hard to say. But now, he was searching.

Part of his problem, though, was that he didn't really know what he was searching for. In his wandering, he met another man who seemed to be wandering too. And they walked together as the one man searched in his lostness.

After a while, he no longer felt lost because, now, he had a Companion for his journey. In time, they came upon a path. It was a narrow path, but it gave the searching man a surge of hope. Now, he felt, surely, his journey would lead him somewhere.

"Which way should we go?" he asked his Companion.

His Companion said, "This way." He trusted his Companion, so in that direction they continued.

The searching man asked his Companion, "Have you been down this path before?"

"Many times," was his answer.

"Tell me where it leads," he implored.

"It leads to the Gate of Suffering."

"Why are you taking me to the Gate of Suffering? I would rather be nowhere than have to suffer!"

"In the other direction, there is nothing."

But do not think of the suffering, think of the glory beyond it. Think of all the kindness, peace, love, and goodness you have known in your life; magnify it a hundred times, and that is what lies beyond the Gate of Suffering."

As he continued to describe the glory that was there, beyond the gate, the lost man seemed to feel hope rising in his heart. He felt a sense of purpose, a reason for living. A look of conviction and determination gleamed in his eyes.

It was as if this was the very thing he was searching for.

In fact, he felt as if he had already found it, just being on the path. He was walking on the Path to Glory! He would see it soon!

"Why is it called the Gate of Suffering?"

"It is called the Gate of Suffering because, long, long ago, a Good Man suffered a great deal in his efforts to open it. The Good Man suffered so much because he wanted to open it not only for himself, but for many others. But because some men doubted that the Good Man could open it, they treated him shamefully; they beat him, and they took his life."

"Did he ever open the gate?"

Before he could answer, at that very moment, the Companion could hear from deep in the woods, far from the path, a desperate cry for help. Quickly leaving the path, the two men followed its sound and ran to give aid. There was a family, hungry, hurting, and lost.

The hopeful man found food for them, and, together, he and the Companion began to walk with them and lead them to the path. After some distance toward the path, they heard more distant cries. The Companion took the hopeful man aside and said that there were many others lost and wandering as he had been.

He felt called to find them and bring them to the path.

He must now leave, and the hopeful man must now be a Companion. But before he left, he told the hopeful man to remember him, and, when he could, to help others find the path.

"Remember the glory!" he said.

"Remember the glory."

The story, at this point, tells of many ventures away from the path taken by the hopeful man, and many returns. Some of his adventures had to do with the struggles of others, some had to do with struggles for justice, and some, many, had to do with temptations that led him from his path. But something kept reminding him that he was to be like the Companion: kind, loving, righteous, a guiding hand.

And so, he did his best.

Near the end of his journey, he met up with his Companion again. Together they walked the final miles until, through the trees, the very tops of the Gateway to Glory could be seen. Just ahead, there was a fork in the path. One branch led toward the gate.

"Where does the other path lead?" asked the hopeful man.

"It leads nowhere," said the Companion.

The hopeful man took the Pathway to Glory, toward the Gate of Suffering. The Companion went with him. The path came around until the gate was in full view, and the hopeful man was curiously amazed, astonished to discover that (slowly) the gate was wide open!

He stopped and looked at his Companion.

"Why is it still called the Gate of Suffering?"

"Because suffering is the Gateway to Glory. The entry into Glory was made long ago by the Good Man, who died trying to open its gate.

But when he died, the gate was soon opened.

The Good Man opened it from the other side!

Yes, he did die, but his suffering defeated evil, and his love defeated death! He rose from death in Glory, and his resurrection opened the gate. And you are welcomed.

"All are welcome to come and pass through into Glory. Even now you stand on the threshold."

This story is about many things. It is about a good man, a searching man, a companion, a path, and the gate of suffering. We are all searching, but because of the good man's example of self-sacrifice, we can all be inspired to be companions. And because of the good man's sacrifice and suffering, we no longer need to suffer, but we can still be self-sacrificing. We can risk leaving the pathway to glory because we know the hope that we can have. And because we know this hope, we can't help but want to share it; we can guide others to the path. We can be servants, servants of the path. Being a servant is a sort of suffering, because in serving, we go out of our way, leave our path at times to be a companion. But if we remain servants of the path, the gate of suffering will remain open for us. We stand, even now, upon the threshold. To follow the path of the companion is to be prepared for the entry into Glory!

Reappearance

While they were talking about this,
Jesus Himself stood among them and said,
"Peace be with you."
They were startled and terrified,
and thought that they were seeing a ghost.
He said to them, "Why are you frightened,
and why do doubts arise in your hearts?
Look at my hands and my feet; see that it is I myself.
Touch me and see;
for a ghost does not have flesh and bones as you see that I have.
And when he had said this, he showed them his hands and feet.
While in their joy they were disbelieving and still wondering,
he said to them, "Have you anything to eat?"
They gave him a piece of broiled fish, and he took it and ate in their presence.

—LUKE 24:36–43

I n the Gospel of Luke, at this point, only three people have seen the resurrected Christ: Peter, Cleopas, and Cleopas's companion in the walk to Emmaus. The latter two had just returned to Jerusalem to tell the other disciples that they had seen the risen Lord. They were greeted by the excited group with the acknowledgment that Jesus had risen indeed, and that Simon Peter had seen Him (a story not told in Luke). While they were telling their friends about their journey to Emmaus, the meal, their recognition of the risen Christ in the breaking of the bread, and His sudden disappearance, suddenly, Jesus appeared! They were startled, at least at first. But Jesus said, "Peace be with you" (Luke 24:36).

But it's kind of hard to compose yourself and feel the peace when you've just been startled. Terror is the more natural reaction to seeing someone alive that you thought was dead. Were they seeing a ghost? The pain of their grief may not have been as sharp on Sunday night as it was on Friday night. By now they would probably be at the earliest stages of acceptance with respect to Jesus's death.

Once the shock of Christ's reappearance was absorbed, probably a good word to describe their emotional state is that they were dumbfounded. "Why are you frightened, and why do doubts rise in your minds?" (v. 38). Why? You just appeared! Out of nowhere! No one ever did anything like that before! Something was happening! It was as out of the ordinary as walking on water! Hmmmm. It was not peace that they felt. They were dumbfounded! He had been crucified! He was dead! He'd been buried! This sort of thing just doesn't happen! They knew there was something extraordinary about Jesus. They had even believed He was the Messiah ... until He'd been crucified and died. Then, they didn't know what to believe. So, they needed some convincing. "Look at my hands and my feet see that it is I myself" (v. 39a). "It's me!" He's saying, "It's really me!" "Touch me and see, for a ghost does not have flesh and bones as you see that I have!" (v. 39b).

Everybody there probably had what you could call their duh-face showing. They're just staring at Jesus, mouths gaping open, eyes bulging ... dumbfounded. It was too good to be true! They couldn't believe their eyes! This was amazing! And then there was what I imagine may have been a dreadfully long, stupefied silence, where it says, in their doubt they were disbelieving and still wondering. Meanwhile, Peter is getting antsier by the second. All he can think, I imagine, is, "See! Look at that! I told you so! Wasn't I right! Isn't this great! I knew it was true!" I picture Cleopas and the other guy nodding with confidence, folding their arms, and wanting to say, "Why didn't you tell us it was You? Why did You disappear? Glad we can see You again ... We wanted to talk to you so much more!" All the rest are slowly getting it. It makes them so happy that they just can't absorb it all. It's just incredible! They're flying! And during that pause, Jesus says something that brings everyone back down to earth. "Got anything to eat?" (24:41 paraphrased).

They gave Him a piece of broiled fish. He took it and ate it in their presence! Ghosts don't eat. Dead people don't eat. But Jesus could eat. He could be touched. He could be embraced. The reunion must have become filled with chatter, with embracing one another, and with joy. It was glorious.

The story makes us wonder, however, about what sort of body Jesus now has. It could appear and disappear. But it still had the wounds of the Crucifixion! It was not quite the same, but He could be recognized! He had died, but He was alive! He was resurrected, but He could still eat! But we forget that Jesus is God! He is supernatural. Jesus is the incarnation of God. And with our natural minds we can't explain it. The good news is that we shouldn't need to. We can simply embrace the wonder and bask in the glory. It is a mystery now, but a time will come for all who believe, who trust, when we will understand fully. For now, let us rejoice. For now, let us embrace the mystery. For now, let us just enjoy this sign of the power of God.

Christ is risen! He is risen indeed!

Is it too hard to take? I can see how it might be. In the wonderful movie *Castaway,* with Tom Hanks and Helen Hunt, Hanks's character survives the crash of a FedEx cargo plane and lives for over five years on a deserted tropical island. Back home, after a while, his fiancée, Hunt, moved on with her life, got married, and had children. When the opportunity came for her to see him after his unexpected return, she just couldn't take it. In her mind, he'd been dead for so long that it was, in a way, somehow, too much for her to embrace. It was not that she couldn't accept that he was alive. It was not that she didn't believe it; it was just too overwhelming for her at first. Some people can't fully embrace what is overwhelming. It takes a lot of faith.

But later, Tom Hanks comes to her. The shock had diminished enough by then for her to absorb it now, and she is then able to embrace him.

Many people seem to choose not to embrace the overwhelming mystery of the resurrection. They water it down to the allegorical, metaphorical, or symbolic. And the result is that they cannot receive any peace of mind about this aspect of their faith: The resurrection. They alter in their minds the meaning of the resurrection, and so they must alter in their minds the meaning of the incarnation, of the atoning sacrifice of Christ on the cross, and of most of what the New Testament says about the Christian faith, the kingdom of God, and the purpose of the church. They may still have a faith they would call Christian, but it is watered down and turned into a powerless series of principles and platitudes.

The risen Christ had said, "Peace be with you." Peace is a wonderful fruit of our faith. It may begin when we accept the truth intellectually, but it is when we believe in our hearts that true peace can begin to be embraced. And peace is not just a sense of relief after grief. It is not just a sense of how everything is okay. It is not just a sense of satisfaction or contentment about life. It is a sense of wholeness, of completeness, of fulfillment. It is a sense of knowing something that surpasses understanding. Only Christ offers this peace.

I have known this peace, but it is allusive. I have felt this peace, but it seems to disappear every time I turn around and see hatred and animosity in the world, or even close to home. I have sought this peace, but there is so much that is left unfulfilled all around me that it is like looking for the living among the dead. But I trust that it will come completely … someday. I pray for peace—mine and yours.

Why Do Doubts Arise in Your Hearts?

While they were talking about this,
Jesus himself stood among them, and said to them,
"Peace be with you."
They were startled and terrified,
and thought that they were seeing a ghost.
He said to them,
"Why are you frightened,
and why do doubts arise in your hearts?
Look at my hands and my feet; see that it is I myself.
Touch me and see;
for a ghost does not have flesh and bones as you see that I have."
And when he had said this, he showed them his hands and his feet.

—LUKE 24:36–40

There is a story from about seven hundred years ago in Eastern Europe of a young man who had become a Christian after hearing about Christ from a Franciscan preacher. His father had recently died in a battle against a pagan city, and his mother had two young daughters. To support them, the young man indentured himself into the service of a nearby feudal lord. They became close, despite the master-servant relationship, and the young man shared his faith with his master. The master accepted Christ, but because of his position and status, did not practice his faith outwardly. To do so, he thought, would undermine his authority. He did become a kinder man, however.

After many years, this lord fell at odds with another lord in a nearby city-state. A turf war ensued; the master was killed, and the young man was placed in a dungeon to await execution. He consoled himself by retelling other captives the story of Christ as he had learned it. None of the men were given any food because, due to their upcoming executions, their keeper said they were already as good as dead. But the keeper overheard some of the stories about Jesus and was particularly touched by both the story of the Crucifixion and the young man's story of selling himself into slavery. The sacrifice he had made on behalf of his mother and sisters seemed very noble, for he too had sisters.

The keeper wanted to hear more, and he began to bring small amounts of food to the several men in the dungeon. When he heard the story of the resurrection, he got an idea. He told the young man that he would tell his master that no executions would be necessary. The captives were all to pretend to be deathly ill. Then, one by one, he would carry out their "lifeless" bodies to be buried. Only once away from the possible sight of his master, he would set them free. Each one felt the power of the resurrection, for whereas before they were as good as dead, now they felt alive again.

The young man insisted on being the last one set free. But the longer he remained, the nearer the possibility of his execution might come. In fact, one night, the Lord announced that his execution would be the next day. The keeper insisted that it was time to feign death to escape execution. The young man agreed only if the keeper would agree to flee his master with him. So it was that the two escaped. Both felt the power of the resurrection. They came to the young man's home. The former keeper, an older man, married the young man's mother; they became carpenters in honor of their savior, and their family prospered in many positive ways.

"Why do questionings rise among you? (Luke 24:38).

The main reason it is so hard to understand is that it is just so incredible! The experience of a dead man come back to life is even rarer than the experience of a change of heart in a hardened jailer. A first reaction is often doubt, even if it is a change of heart. "See my hands and my feet? It's really me!" (v. 39). The proof of the power of the resurrection is a changed life. But we sometimes resist this power because we settle for what we are. We've gotten used to this way of being. To let ourselves be changed would seem like work. On the other hand, the freedom to be gained is worth the change.

"'These are my words, which I spoke to you, while I was still with you, that everything written about me in the Law of Moses and the prophets and the Psalms must be fulfilled.' Then he opened their minds to understand" (vv. 44–45). With Easter faith comes an opened mind, a mind willing to accept not just the truth, but what it can mean in our own lives. Understanding comes even in the midst of troubled hearts, anxious minds, and questionings rising. An awareness comes of a larger picture. A respect comes for the deeper meaning in life.

What is curious to me is the scars on Jesus's hands and feet. If Jesus was able to live again, and even eat again, something must have mended. His pierced heart had started to beat again. His lifeless limbs must have somehow had new blood coursing through their veins, for He had practically bled to death. Healing must have happened in a very remarkable way—in a very glorious way. But if there was that degree of healing, why the scars?

Unless … unless His body was not healed. The slight difference between healing and resurrection might very well be the scars. Jesus's body didn't come *back* to life; it was given new life. It was a real body. It was the same body, but the life in it, its aliveness, was not earthly anymore. The divine nature, the Holy Spirit, was its only life now. The flesh, though real, and, living, was not earthly anymore. Jesus had been changed. We too shall be changed.

Jesus said that "in the resurrection, they are like the angels in heaven" (Matthew 22:30). We do not become angels, but we become *like* angels—spiritual beings, not perishable flesh. Jesus's physical body, though not different, had been changed. "Flesh and blood cannot inherit the Kingdom of God, nor does the perishable the imperishable! Lo! I tell you a mystery: We shall not all sleep, but we shall all be changed, in a moment, in the twinkling of an eye, at the last trumpet!" (1 Corinthians 15:50–52).

Paul said, several verses earlier, "What you sow does not come to life unless it dies. And what you sow is not the body which is to be." (1 Corinthians 15:36–37).

Another reason questionings may rise is that it all still remains a mystery. The resurrection can only be understood by the human mind as a change comparable to, but much more amazing than, a change of heart in a human life.

Jesus said to his disciples: "Thus it is written, that the Christ should suffer and on the third day rise from the dead, and that repentance and forgiveness of sins should be preached in His name to all nations, beginning from Jerusalem. You are witnesses of these things" (Luke 24:46–48). Today, we may not be witnesses of changed hearts as much as of changed lives!

Fulfillment

Then He said to them,
"These are my words that I spoke to you while I was still with you—
that everything written about me in the law of Moses,
the prophets, and the psalms must be fulfilled."
Then he opened their minds to understand the scriptures,
and he said to them, "Thus it is written,
that the Messiah is to suffer
and to rise from the dead on the third day,
and that repentance and forgiveness of sins
is to be proclaimed in his name to all nations,
beginning from Jerusalem.
You are witnesses of these things.
And see, I am sending you what my Father promised;
so stay here in the city
until you have been clothed with power from on high."
Then he led out as far as Bethany,
and, lifting up his hands, he blessed them.
While he was blessing them, he withdrew from them
and was carried up into heaven.
And they worshiped him,
and returned to Jerusalem with great joy;
and they were continually in the temple blessing God.

—LUKE 24:44–53

Everything written (Luke 44c) about me in the Law of Moses—Genesis, Exodus, Leviticus, Numbers, and Deuteronomy, Everything written in the Prophets … (44d), the rest of the Old Testament except the histories, Esther, Job, Psalms, Proverbs, and Ecclesiastes—and, everything written in the Psalms (44e) … must be fulfilled! Everything? Israel was supposed to be restored by the Messiah! Evil was supposed to end! The enemies of God were supposed to be eliminated! These things have not been fulfilled yet! Sometimes those words of prophecy are interpreted as allegorical sayings and thought to be meant more as spiritual forecasts. The restoration of Israel is supposed to mean a restoration of faith rather than of a nation. The defeat of evil has supposedly happened on a spiritual level of some kind. And the elimination of God's enemies … well, the only real enemy of God is Satan, and Satan is envisioned as being eliminated in the Revelation. Again, it is seen by many scholars as something allegorical or spiritual rather than literal and actual.

But if the scriptures about the Messiah as the suffering servant are claimed as having been literally fulfilled by Jesus, then we should probably expect the rest to be fulfilled as well. But even Jesus proclaimed that these would be fulfilled sometime in the future. Though Jesus had said, "It is finished," in John 19:30, He has also said He would come again in the Revelation to John (22:20). The Gospels in Matthew 24, Mark 13, and Luke 21 all mention the Second Coming, but it is after a great tribulation. It is spoken of in the book of Acts, and it is angels who tell the disciples, after Jesus had ascended, "This Jesus, who has been taken from you into heaven, will come in the same way as you saw Him go into heaven!" (Acts 1:11). Before that, the disciples had asked, "Lord, is this the time when you will restore the Kingdom of Israel?" And Jesus said, "It is not for you to know the times or periods that the Father has set by His own authority" (1:6–7). He implies, then, that it *will* happen. And some believe that Israel was already restored in 1948. But the kingdom on which Jesus focused in His preaching was not an earthly realm, but the kingdom of heaven.

Some of Paul's letters talk about the Second Coming, but there was an immanence to his expectations. And the fact is that Christ's literal Second Coming has still not yet happened. Still, we should be ready. And this was taught as a matter of faith, not a matter of earthly preparations for the arrival or a fulfilment of an earthly kingdom. Many think the Second Coming could happen anytime. But we must acknowledge that though not everything written about the Messiah in the Hebrew scriptures has happened, everything necessary had happened.

If the whole Jewish nation and the Gentiles had believed in Jesus, not only would they have been redeemed from sin, but the rest would have followed as well. You see, once sin was taken care of, and true belief was established in the hearts of all people, a kingdom of faith would have been established, evil would have been defeated, and love would have eliminated the perception of others as enemies. The picture of what was to come into focus was that of a "brotherhood of man under the Fatherhood of God." But many people believe. Jesus must have known this would be the case, and perhaps it was a part of God's eternal plan, because the real issue is faith not nation. The real issue is belief not race. The real issue is love not power.

Jesus opened their minds to understand the scriptures, and said to them, "Thus it is written that the Messiah is to suffer and to rise from the dead on the third day" (v. 46). Many verses of scripture, especially in Isaiah, forecast a suffering savior. It is in Hosea where the resurrection imagery is foreseen: "Come, let us return to the Lord; for it is He who has torn, and He will heal us; He has struck down, and He will bind us up. After two days He will revive us; on the third day He will raise us up, that we may live before Him" (Hosea 6:10).

But after Jesus reiterates this prophecy, He then says, "and that repentance and forgiveness of sins is to be proclaimed to all nations" (47). Prophetic scriptures are rife with calls to repentance and the promise of forgiveness. The hard part, due to a sort of nationalistic pride, is that it is to be proclaimed to all nations. But Jesus told them: "Beginning from Jerusalem, you are witnesses of these things" (v. 48). It is like He is saying, "Starting from here with you," the whole world will hear it.

Then Jesus made a very particular promise: "Behold (See), I am sending upon you what my Father promised; so stay here in the city until you have been clothed with power from on high!" (49). And we know what happened seven weeks later! They were filled with the Holy Spirit. They were set on fire, and that fire began to spread! And it should still be spreading. The problem is that people are afraid to burn. There's a poem I once wrote that ends by saying,

But blazes die, and embers cool,

And life becomes a search for fuel.

(Tom Kingery, "A Face Among the Flames")

What we don't realize is that the fire of faith is self-perpetuating. The more it burns, the more it is fueled.

Stay here, Jesus said. Wait. There is a contemporary rock song that reminds us that "the waiting is the hardest part!" Unless, that is, you know how to wait. Pay attention to how the Gospel of Luke ends. Jesus "led them out as far as Bethany, and lifting His hands, He blessed them … While He was blessing them, He withdrew from them and was carried up into heaven" (50–51). This blessing was not the final blessing. This is still Sunday night. Just that morning, Jesus had risen. But this blessing is, to the disciples, without a doubt, a heavenly blessing.

Then what? "And they worshiped Him" (52a) … the waiting had begun, but there was worship was in their waiting. "And they returned to Jerusalem … with great joy; and, they were continually in the temple blessing God" (53). The power would come. But for now, there was worship in their hearts. It was continual. It was visible—in the temple. It was corporate—they were together. And it was filled with blessing and joy.

The way to wait for the power to come was in worship. The power to come was meant for every disciple. The fire of Pentecost can be ignited in every believer's heart. But the power does not come to those who do not worship!

PART 5
The Resurrection in John

The following meditations are inspired by passages from the Gospel of John. Not every thought here derives from a resurrection story about Jesus, but when Jesus says, "I am the resurrection and the life ..." (John 11:25), there is a reason to feel that the words are thought-worthy for the subject of this book. John is more detailed than the synoptic Gospels at some points, at other turns, scenes are less clear. Only Mary Magdalene comes to the tomb at dawn. There's a lot of running in John. After Peter and "the other disciple" leave the scene, there is a beautiful encounter between the risen Christ and Mary Magdalene. She was the first person to see Jesus risen from the dead. But I want to start with the wonderful scene of the resurrection of Lazarus from chapter 11. It sets the stage in some ways for understanding Christ's own resurrection.

I Am the Resurrection and the Life

"Our friend Lazarus has fallen asleep, but I am going to awaken him."
The disciples said to him, "Lord, if he has fallen asleep, he will be all right."
Jesus, however, had been speaking about his death,
but they thought that he was referring merely to sleep.
Then Jesus told them plainly, "Lazarus is dead.
For your sake I am glad I was not there, so that you may believe.
But let us go to him."
Thomas, who was called the Twin, said to his fellow disciples,
"Let us also go, that we may die with him."

When Jesus arrived,
he found that Lazarus had already been in the tomb four days.
Now Bethany was near Jerusalem, some two miles away,
and many of the Jews had come to Martha and Mary
to console them about their brother.
When Martha heard that Jesus was coming,
she went and met him, while Mary stayed at home.
Martha said to Jesus,
"Lord, if you had been here, my brother would not have died.
But even now I know that God will give you whatever you ask of him."
Jesus said to her,
"Your brother will rise again."
Martha said to him, "I know that he will rise again
in the resurrection on the last day."
Jesus said,
"I am the resurrection and the life.
Those who believe in me, even though they die, will live!
And everyone who lives and believes in me will never die.
Do you believe this?"

—JOHN 11:11–26

Years ago, the story was told of how two days had passed since a mine shaft collapsed. The one miner caught in the cave-in had long ceased calling out for help. The air had become stale and thin. His body was weak. All he could do was strike the wall with his hammer, making a faint tapping noise that could be detected by the frantically working rescue team. But his tapping was becoming less and less frequent.

He had urgently prayed since the moment disaster struck. His prayers had first included asking God to just let them know he was down there. After a while, he gave up praying for a real rescue. He knew how deep he was. It would take too long for them to get to him while he was alive. He had been through the bargaining hours, telling God what he would do if only he could live. He couldn't let himself sleep. The breaths he would be taking would be too deep. He'd use up his air all the sooner. He needed to maintain shallow breathing to save as much good air as possible. Something inside him kept him striking the wall with his hammer. He felt as though he was as good as dead. He used his hammer one last time, and then he let himself drift off to sleep. And he dreamed. He dreamed about his family, his parents, his wife, his children, and his friends. And he dreamed that they were all there. They were all holding hammers, tapping. … tapping … tapping!

The tapping was not a dream. With a surge of energy, he raised his hammer and struck the wall. His tapping was returned by a whole lot of good, solid taps. The rescue had come. And he was saved. He felt born again!

"Very truly, I tell you, unless a grain of wheat falls into the earth and dies, it remains just a single grain; but if it dies, it bears much fruit" (John 12:24).

It seems strange that Jesus could be so mistaken! Paul said practically the same thing (1 Corinthians 15:36). "What you sow does not come to life unless it dies." A seed that dies, however, is the seed that remains alone. That never gets planted. In time, it will only rot. The seed must germinate to grow, to sprout, to produce its fruit. It does not die. It is transformed. It is changed. It can no longer be easily recognized as a seed. What was once just a seed becomes roots growing down into the earth, and a shoot bursting upwards through the soil. But the seed is gone. Gone!

Jesus and Paul, though, are teaching a lesson about the resurrection, not about botany. The resurrection is the transformation that can happen only when there has been death.

The miner trapped in the cave didn't die, he was saved. Being rescued was like being born again. He had fallen into the earth the way the seed must fall into the earth. But somehow, the miner was transformed, the way the seed must be transformed. Being rescued was like being raised from the dead. And being born again is like being resurrected.

Jesus Christ is the grain of wheat that died to bear much fruit. Jesus Christ died for us. We no longer need to die; we become transformed. I said that the resurrection is the transformation that can happen only when there has been a death. And it is *His* death that bears the fruit of our transformation. Jesus said, "I am the resurrection and the life; anyone who believes in me, though they die, yet shall they live!" (John 11:25).

Lazarus had believed. Jesus said to Martha, "Your brother will rise again" (v. 23). Martha believed only in a resurrection at the end of time. This was the common belief of their day. But Jesus knew it was a matter of faith and power. Lazarus had the faith; Jesus had the power.

Lazarus's resurrection is not a resuscitation. He was not revived. He was raised from the dead. Yes, because he was mortal, and his risen life was still in this world, he would again have to die, but his faith would bring him life in the world to come. His belief in Jesus as the savior would make an everlasting difference. His relationship with the one whose death would transform death, would see him through to new life in God's kingdom, in heaven.

It is this that transforms us now and sets the treasure of our hearts within heaven's realm. This power, this relationship, this faith. One of the stories about John Wesley, the founder of Methodism, is how he rode in the gallows cart with a man condemned to die, whom he had come to visit in the London prison. Through the visits Wesley had shared with the man, I believe he was a thief—he found him very remorseful. Wesley led him to repentance. The man feared death because he was certain he was going to hell. But Wesley did his best to reassure him that if he truly put his trust in Jesus, and believed in him, he would yet live. The man truly grieved his sins, was serving his penitence, and prayed for God to forgive him. The man confessed his faith in Jesus as his Lord and savior. And now he was riding in the gallows cart. His hands were tied. His heart was racing because he still feared death and … hell. But John Wesley told him about the thief on the cross beside Jesus who simply pleaded for Jesus to remember him. Wesley begged the man to fix his sights on paradise.

Another man who was with Wesley saw a notable change come over the condemned man. His body began to relax. His face began to bear a beautiful contentment. Hope welled up in his heart. He had begun to feel an assurance of God's absolute unconditional love for him, He felt redeemed, and he began to feel what Paul felt in Philippians (1:21, 23): "to live is Christ, and to die is gain … My desire is to depart and be with Christ, for that is far better." Wesley had also taught him this truth. The man's fear of death vanished. Now he only had hope and wanted to meet his maker. He felt reborn. He felt triumphant. Though he truly was guilty of his crimes, he knew his sins were forgiven now. He knew that though he would die, yet he would live. Because … he believed! His last words, granted by his executioners, were his confession of faith—his testimonial witness to the transforming power of faith in Jesus Christ.

Like the miner hearing his tapping returned, he felt like a new man. It was still an hour or so before the miner was up on the surface, but he felt rescued already.

We can know the power of the resurrection today! It can work in us now, transforming us by the renewal of our minds, giving us a certitude with Martha that we will rise again in the resurrection of the last day! And because of this, through Christ and in Christ as we rise up from the death of sin, a righteous morality can come alive in our hearts. Our thoughts move us beyond ourselves to the building of God's kingdom here and now, to seeking and doing God's will on earth as it is done in heaven. Our zeal for service is revived, our efforts in mission are resuscitated, and our desire to please God burns like a great light within us. It's as if a seed of truth has germinated, and the flower of faith has blossomed. It's as if a new light has begun to shine in the darkness of this world, like a breath of fresh air has come to our lungs, and a cleansing tide has washed over us, and we feel all the more loved, and all the more loving.

And so, despite the darkness, we keep tapping. Despite our human guilt, we keep hoping. Despite our death, we keep believing. Jesus is the resurrection and the life. The one who conquered death by dying and brings us life by rising, has given us a gift—everlasting life!

The Raising of Lazarus

Jesus said to her,
"I am the resurrection and the life.
Those who believe in me, even though they die, will live.
And everyone who lives and believes in me will never die.
Do you believe this?"

She [Martha] said to him, "Yes, Lord,
I believe that you are the Messiah of God, the one who is coming into the world."

When she had said this, she went back and called her sister Mary,
and told her privately, "The Teacher is here and is calling for you."
And when she heard it, she got up quickly and went to him.
Now Jesus had not yet come to the village,
but was still at the place where Martha had met him.
The Jews who were with her in the house, consoling her,
saw Mary get up quickly and go out.
They followed her
because they thought that she was going to the tomb to weep there.
When Mary came to where Jesus was and saw him,
she knelt at his feet and said to him,
"Lord, if you had been here, my brother would not have died."
When Jesus saw her weeping,
and the Jews who came with her also weeping,
he was greatly disturbed in spirit and deeply moved.
He said, "Where have you laid him?"
They said to him, "Lord, come and see."

Jesus began to weep.

So the Jews said, "See how he loved him!"
But some of them said,
"Could not he who opened the eyes of the blind man have kept this man from dying?"

Then Jesus, again greatly disturbed, came to the tomb.
It was a cave, and a stone was lying against it.
Jesus said,
"Take away the stone."

Martha, the sister of the dead man, said to him,
"Lord, already there is a stench
because he has been dead four days."
Jesus said to her,
"Did I not tell you that if you believed, you would see the glory of God?"
So they took away the stone.
And Jesus looked upward and said,
"Father, I thank you for having heard me.
I knew that you always hear me,
but I have said this for the sake of the crowd standing here,
so that they may believe that you sent me."
When he had said this, he cried with a loud voice,
"Lazarus, come out!"

The dead man came out,
his hands and feet bound with strips of cloth,
and his face wrapped in a cloth.
Jesus said to them,
"Unbind him, and let him go."

—JOHN 11:25–44

Think for a moment of the parable of the prodigal son. Think of the father in that story. Think about the remarkable way he seemed to have been hoping for his son's return. He had wonderful memories of the young man as a boy. He would have remembered holding him as an infant, playing with him as a toddler, watching his first steps, seeing him begin to play, celebrating his birthdays, his triumphs, and dealing with his struggles as a teenager, and his entrance into manhood. Parents remember all of this. To us our children are not just adults when they grow up; they are the total of every year they have lived. When his son left home, to the father, it was as if his son had died.

When I was a child, I grew up next door to the Nelsons. They were an ancient couple. They still drove a 1940s vintage Pontiac. (Of course, at that time it was only twenty years old.) And in many ways, we all took care of them. The boys mowed their lawn, my dad did some of their gardening. And my mom, after Mr. Nelson died, visited Ovida (Wid) almost every day, and occasionally drove her around. But when I was sixteen, we moved away. My mom still did a lot for Mrs. Nelson. And one day during my college years, when I was the only one at home, Mrs. Nelson called. She was distressed about something and wanted my mom to come over. I think it had something to do with her housekeeper. I told her she was not at home right then. And I asked her if I could come over to help her. She said yes, please. After being there for a while, I found out that all she needed was for someone to be with her. She didn't have anything for me to do. In fact, she didn't even remember me. She was simply comforted by knowing that I was my mother's son.

I told her that I remembered Mr. Nelson. She didn't know that I did. So, I asked her to tell me about him. His name was Victor. Her memories took her way back, long before the Second World War. She told me what he did for a living, how they met, and where they had lived before coming to Pine Street in Winnetka. She even spoke some Swedish for some reason. The amazing thing about the conversation was the way it brought her to life. And I learned something important. She told me that remembering Victor made her feel like he was alive again, even though saying that brought a tear to her eye.

After about an hour had passed, I saw my mom drive by, (we had moved three blocks away). In a few minutes, I phoned her to let her know I was at Mrs. Nelson's house, and could she come over. She was there in a minute or two, and I let her take over. She is the one Mrs. Nelson really wanted to be there. But she was very grateful I had come.

Our memories can make it seem like the one we've lost is alive again! The prodigal father even said, "This, my son was lost and is found, he was dead and is alive again!" (Luke 15:24) All the memories, all the experiences of his son were even more real now that the boy was home. Jesus gives us a new way of looking at life. The life we live is just a momentary blip in the grand scheme of things. We should not live for this life but for the life to come. Because that life is everlasting! But Jesus also gives us a new way of looking at death.

Jesus is the resurrection and the life. Consider this: Is there anything between you and God? Any barriers? Think about it. What separates you from God? Listen to what Paul said in Romans 8:35, 37–39:

> Who shall separate us from the love of Christ? Shall tribulation, or distress, or persecution, or famine, or nakedness, or peril, or sword? … No, in all these things we are more than conquerors through Him who loved us. For I am sure that neither death, nor life, nor angels, nor principalities, nor things present, nor things to come, nor powers, nor height, nor depth, nor anything else in all creation, will be able to separate us from the love of God in Christ Jesus our Lord!

Not even death can separate us from God! We who are Christians, who believe in and follow Jesus Christ, can understand death differently than the world.

Think of what death means. For most people, it is a threat to life, and to the living. Death is a threat to our sense of security. The prodigal son felt security with his big inheritance, but he lost it. Death is something over which we often feel we have no control. The prodigal son thought he was in control, but he lost it. Death leaves us all feeling a bit vulnerable. And the prodigal son confronted that vulnerability. In the medical field, death is often seen as a failure. Something didn't work. Some life-sustaining and life-enhancing treatment didn't succeed. But for the prodigal son, his failures led him to a chance to start over. He learned that if you play it too cool, you turn to ice.

Death is not our enemy. Fear is the enemy! We fear the unknown. We cannot feel secure before the unknowns in our lives. We cannot control the unknown. We are vulnerable before all that is unknown. To die is to lose life. Death is sad. To die is to leave life. Death is lonely. To die is to end life. Death is frustrating because so often it comes when life still seems unfinished. We always feel as though it has interrupted life somehow. Jesus said, "I am the resurrection and the life, they who believe in me, though they die, yet shall they live. And whoever lives and believes in me, shall never die" (John 11:25).

Never die? It depends on how you define death. Death, as I shared previously, is, to Christians, a transformation. It is not an end but a new beginning. We have the promise of the resurrection at the end of time. That's the "yet shall they live" reality. But we also have the promise of eternal life. Belief is the qualifier for both. If we live, and have eternal life, we do not die. Our mortal bodies will have an end to them. The life in these bodies will be finished some. day. But hear these words from Paul's Letter to the Romans:

> We know that our old self was crucified with Him so that the body of sin might be destroyed, and we might no longer be enslaved to sin. For they who have died are freed from sin. But if we have died with Christ we believe that we shall also live with Him. For we know that Christ being raised from the dead will never die again; death no longer has dominion over Him. The death He died He died to sin, once for all; but the life He lives He lives to God. So you also must consider yourselves dead to sin and alive to God in Christ Jesus. (Romans 6:6–11)

Death no longer has dominion! We see our death differently because of our relationship to Jesus Christ. And though death seems to have a grip on the world, we can see beyond this world. Someone once said that to get to the kingdom of sunshine and rainbows, you need to learn to see in the dark. Such is the effect of our faith. We can see through the darkness of this world. The highway starts low. To get higher, go deep. Discover the new way of looking at death. Death has no victory. Death has no sting. For the sting of death is sin (1 Corinthians 15:55–56). Death is not final. We believe in giving glory to God; as it was in the beginning, it is now, and ever shall be world without end! "Thanks be to God, who gives us the victory through our Lord Jesus Christ!" (1 Corinthians 15:57).

Because He lives, death has been defeated, conquered, overcome. "Death has been swallowed up in victory!" (1 Corinthians 15:54 and Isaiah 25:8). "Death no longer has dominion over Jesus! The death He died, He died to sin, once for all; but the life he lives, He lives to God. So we also must consider ourselves dead to sin and alive to God in Christ Jesus" (Romans 6:9–11).

Those Who Believe in Me Will Live

"Those who believe in me. ... will live!"
—JOHN 11:25C

Sometimes the best way to interpret a passage of scripture is by looking at other scriptures.

Paul said, in his Letter to the Romans:

> If we have been united with Him in a Death like His, we
> will certainly be united with Him in a resurrection like
> His. We know that our old self was crucified with Him
> so that the body of sin might be destroyed, and we might
> no longer be enslaved to sin. For whoever has died is freed
> from sin. But if we have died with Christ, we believe that
> we will also live with Him. We know that Christ, being
> raised from the dead, will never die again; death no longer
> has dominion over Him. The Death He died, He died to
> sin, once for all; but the Life He lives He lives to God So
> you also must consider yourselves dead to sin and alive to
> God in Christ Jesus. (6:5–11)

When we begin to believe, sin in us begins to die. We become "dead to sin and alive to God in Christ Jesus" (Romans 6:11). We are changed. But faith doesn't stop there. God isn't finished with us. As long as we are still in this world, God is never finished with us! We need to be united with Jesus in His death!

The love of Christ urges us on, because we are convinced that one has died for all; therefore all have died. And He died for all, so that those who live might live no longer for themselves, but for Him who died and was raised for them. From now on, therefore, we regard no one from a human point of view. (2 Corinthians 5:14–16)

We have already died … died to sin … if we are in Christ!

If anyone is in Christ, there is a new creation; everything old has passed away; behold, everything has become new! (2 Corinthians 5:17)

For our sake, God made Him to be sin who knew no sin, so that in Him we might become the righteousness of God! (2 Corinthians 5:21)

All because we are dead to sin and alive to God in Christ Jesus!

By grace Jesus raised Lazarus. By the power of life within Him, He brought life to Lazarus! The grace Jesus offered to Mary and Martha by raising their brother Lazarus from death brought them life as well. Grace always enlivens, makes life better, more, greater. "Those who live and believe in me will never die!" (John 11:26). It makes life eternal!

This is a promise that does no less than give us hope. It gives us an assurance that in Christ there is a power that not only raises us up to eternity in some sweet bye and bye but that positions us, spiritually, in life … in eternity. But something must die. There is no resurrection if there is no death. What has died in those who believe is sin—original sin. Remember that "if anyone is in Christ, there is a new creation" (2 Corinthians 5:17).

I have been crucified with Christ; it is no longer I who live but it is Christ who lives in me. And the life I now live in the flesh, I live by faith in the Son of God who loved me and gave Himself for me. (Galatians 2:19b-20)

I have been crucified with Christ! It is a spiritual reality that begins when we begin to believe. And remember: "If we have been united with Him in a Death like His, we will certainly be united with Him in a resurrection like His." (Romans 6:5)

Firstborn among Many

*We know that all things work together for good
for those who love God,
who are called according to his purpose.
For those whom he foreknew
he also predestined to be conformed to the image of his Son,
in order that he might be the firstborn in a large family.
And those whom he predestined he also called;
and those whom he called he also justified
and those whom he justified he also glorified.
We know that all things work together for good for those who
love God, who are called according to his purpose.
For those whom he foreknew
he also predestined to be conformed to the image of his Son,
in order that he might be the firstborn within a large family.
And those whom he predestined he also called;
and those whom he called he also justified,
and those whom he justified he also glorified.*

—ROMANS 8:28–30

D o we look like our picture?

Zan Holmes tells the story of how he flew to a city where he was going to speak at a large gathering, and someone was going to meet him at the airport terminal. He was standing along the wall of the concourse waiting for someone to acknowledge him and connect with him as his ride to the hotel. One man began to approach him, but as he got close, he shook his head and turned to look elsewhere. He kept looking at something in his hand and then at the people nearby. Finally, he went up to Zan Holms, held up the photo in his hand, and asked him, "Is this you?"

"Why, yes it is!" he said with a smile.

And then the man said, "I'm sorry I didn't recognize you. You just don't look like your picture."

Do we look like our picture?

"Those whom God foreknew He also predestined to be confirmed to the likeness of His Son!" (Romans 8:29a). Do we look like our picture—do we have the likeness of God's Son?

I've gone many places in my life, and it is amazing how often people have said that I look like someone. (Even Rick Sutcliffe! He pitched for the Cubs back around 1985, and we're about the same age.) In some way or another, I conform to their likeness. Do we have about us the likeness of those who love God, who are called according to His purpose?" (v. 28). Does it seem like we were "predestined," meant to be what we are? Does it seem like we are called, justified, glorified? Do we look like our picture?

Do we fit into the family of Christ? Even though it might be by adoption that we have become heirs with Him, do we look like we belong in His family picture? Is there any resemblance? Do we look like followers of the One who lived for righteousness, who died for the sins of the world, and who rose in victory over death? If we look like our picture, then we will know that in all things God works for good (8:28) in our lives! And then that will become a part of our picture. That optimism will become our posture and our attitude toward the things that happen in our lives … even the things that seem contrary to "what is good."

Some of the negative things may even be helping us to conform to the likeness of Christ. And though I am not too high on the idea of predestination, or, of certain things being predestined, I must admit that, at times, it just feels as though what has come to be was meant to be.

When Paul uses the word *foreknew* here, I believe it needs to be connected to the word *adoption* in verse 23. Adoption is a very deliberate choice. And God chooses us, when we choose Jesus. This is what is foreknown! And as we choose Jesus every day, we are becoming more and more conformed to His likeness so that, by God's purpose for us, He might be "the firstborn among many brothers and sisters" (v. 29). God wants Jesus to be our brother, our older brother. He is the firstborn, the primary heir, and yet, God makes us His coheirs (Romans 8:17a) when we "share in His suffering in order that we may also share in His glory" (v. 17b).

When it is Easter, we celebrate the glory—the glory of the resurrection. On Easter Sunday, we proclaim that we are Easter people, resurrection people! Do we look like our picture? Is Jesus firstborn in your heart? First in your lives? First in your hopes?

Let's shift gears a moment and focus on the beginning of this passage: "We know that in all things God works for the good of those who love Him! Do we believe this? Do we look like our picture? Do we believe that in the suffering of Jesus, God was working for what is good? Yes! In the death of His Son, God was working for what is good. In His burial, in the sadness of the Passion, in the grief of the disciples, in the confusion of Mary at the tomb, God was working for what is good. Yes! Yes at every point! Then couldn't God be working for what is good through all the things that are happening in your life? Yes … *if*… If we truly love God, if we are called according to His purpose, if we are conformed to the likeness of His Son, and if we are justified! And now, know this: when all those ifs are true in us, we will also be glorified! Do we look like our picture?

Not yet! But God's not finished with any of us yet. There are still a few brush strokes He needs to add to the picture. There are highlights and shadows that still need to be drawn before the picture is complete. You see, there can be no perfect joy without Christ's perfect suffering. There can be no resurrection without a death. We cannot awaken until we realize that we've been sleeping. Mary's confusion works for the good because it serves us. She didn't understand, not at first. But she had an encounter. She saw the Lord, and yet, she was told not to hold on to Him. We know that the dark deed of Christ's Crucifixion worked for the good of the whole world because He was suffering for our sin, in our place, taking the stain of my sin and the pain of my guilt on Himself, so that I could be set free. All the things that happened in the story of Christ's death and resurrection work for our good. His burial tells us that He was truly dead. But His resurrection reveals that His death was truly a part of God's purpose. It was part of God's plan for our salvation. And now, in all the things that are happening in our lives, God is using them to make a picture of us that conforms to the likeness of His Son! We too can make a sacrifice on behalf of others; and we too can experience new life when we do.

The blessings we bring into the lives of others bless us.

Do we look like our picture? Will we look like resurrection people … tomorrow?

MEDITATION 45

The Tomb

_____

After these things, Joseph of Arimathea,
who was a disciple of Jesus,
though a secret one because of his fear of the Jews,
asked Pilate to let him take away the body of Jesus.
Pilate gave him permission;
so he came and removed his body.
Nicodemus, who had at first come to Jesus by night,
also came, bringing a mixture of myrrh and aloes, about a hundred pounds.
They took the body of Jesus and wrapped it with the spices in linen cloths,
according to the burial custom of the Jews.
Now there was a garden in the place where he was crucified,
and in the garden there was a new tomb in which no one had ever been laid.
And so, because it was the Jewish day of Preparation,
and the tomb was nearby,
they laid Jesus there.

—JOHN 19:38–42

T he dead body of Jesus was buried. The Jewish custom included the use of a mixture of myrrh and aloes, not for embalming, but to stifle the scent of death a bit. The use of about one hundred pounds of myrrh and aloes is remarkable because it is the amount that would be used for the burial of a very wealthy man. Using linen cloths also becomes an extravagant expense and would not have been used for criminals. The Gospel of Mark tells us that Joseph of Arimathea bought the shroud for Jesus's burial that day! Some scholars speculate, because the Gospel of Matthew tells us that the tomb was Joseph of Arimathea's own new tomb, that he was expecting to die fairly soon and had spared no expense in his preparations. The tomb, being in a garden area, would have been in the backyard of a very wealthy family.

What little is revealed about Joseph of Arimathea seems to indicate that he had been deeply touched by Christ somehow. He was a Jewish leader, who, for fear of the Jews, felt he could only be a disciple secretly, until now. The risk seems over, and he exposes his faith, and so does Nicodemus, as they arrange for the burial of Jesus's body. The Gospel of John tells nothing of the need to guard the tomb, let alone to set a seal upon it. That story is only in Matthew!

Although there is the impression of haste, John does tell that the burial custom of the Jews was followed. So, we presume that things must have fallen into place fairly quickly, because the burial had to happen before the setting of the sun, and the Day of Passover had begun, which would have lasted from Friday evening to the setting of the sun on Saturday. Because of this, we imagine the closing of the tomb occurring as the sun is going down, and Joseph and Nicodemus returning to their homes in the silent darkness of the Sabbath rest, unclean and therefore unable to go to the temple in the morning because of their having touched a dead body.

The tomb … The one they believed in had been buried. There lay the source of their hopes and the inspiration of their faith. There lay the silenced voice of compassion and the wisdom of the truth.

There lay the one who could heal by His touch and love with His words. All that Jesus meant, in some respects, was buried with Him. And that's why the graves of the ones we love seem to be an important place to visit. Because there our memories unfold, and the meaning of their life returns to us. And even though we know that that meaning is not in this spot where the remains exist, the burial site can still be an important place of remembrance.

Darcie Sims, a grief counselor and author who had lost a young child to the cruel disease of cancer, tells a story about a weekend workshop held for members of an organization called Compassionate Friends. It was particularly for all those who had children who had been killed violently by murder or by drunken drivers. On everyone's nametag was also the name and age of the child who had died.

One woman had been deeply touched by one of Darcie's talks and spoke to her personally during some free time about her grief. The woman was in her late forties, and the age of her daughter had been six when she died. It had obviously been a long time ago, and the woman's grief still seemed fresh. Darcie asked her, "Tell me about your daughter." And the woman spoke about the murder, when it happened, where it happened, how her daughter had been found, and all about the beautiful funeral that had been held.

After many minutes, Darcie asked again, "Tell me about your daughter." And the woman spoke about the murderer, the trial, the jury, the conviction. She shared what she knew about the prison he was in and a little about his daily routine. After several more minutes of listening, Darcie said, "Tell me, what color were your daughter's eyes?" The woman fell apart, buried her head in Darcie's shoulder, and cried, sobbing, "I can't remember."

After they cried together for several minutes, Darcie asked if the woman had a picture. Picking through her purse, she found her wallet. Slowly, she opened it up and found a picture. Taking it out of the blurry old plastic cover, the tears began to flow again as they saw the little girl's face. Finally, the woman said, "They were blue."

There will be reminders of the meaning of the life that's been lost that encourage us. And there will be reminders that perpetuate our grief. All the morbid remembrances of the bloody death of Christ give meaning to our lives only insofar as we keep before us the realization that His death is our death. His suffering is our suffering. And as we face His tomb in silence, we remember not only the life of Jesus who was buried there, but who, on the third day, by God's awesome and mysterious power, was resurrected as Christ, overcoming death, conquering the grave, and opening to us the glory of eternal life. For His resurrection is our resurrection!

Convicted and Called

When it was evening on that day, the first day of the week,
and the doors of the house where the disciples had met
were locked for fear of the Jews,
Jesus came and stood among them and said,
"Peace be with you."
After he said this, he showed them his hands and side.
Then the disciples rejoiced when they saw the Lord.
Jesus said to them again,
"Peace be with you.
As the Father has sent me, so I send you."
When he had said this, he breathed on them and said to them,
"Receive the Holy Spirit.
If you forgive the sins of any, they are forgiven;
if you retain the sins of any they are retained."
But Thomas (who was called the Twin), one of the twelve,
was not with them when Jesus came.
So the other disciples told him, "We have seen the Lord."
But he said to them, "Unless I see the mark of the nails in his hands,
and put my finger in the mark of the nails and my hand in his side,
I will not believe."
A week later
his disciples were again in the house, and Thomas was with them.
Although the doors were shut,
Jesus came and stood among them and said,
"Peace be with you."
Then he said to Thomas,
"Put your finger here and see my hands.
Reach out your hand and put it in my side.
Do not doubt but believe."
Thomas answered him,
"My Lord and my God!"
Jesus said to him,
"Have you believed because you have seen me?
Blessed are those who have not seen and yet have come to believe."

—JOHN 20:19–29

Thomas wanted proof. He was being very objective. He was not thinking of belief as much as he was thinking of his doubts. He was not thinking from the perspective of faith. He was thinking from the perspective of a jurist seeking evidence. He had begun already to completely forget the relationship he had had with Jesus. Now, he just wanted a relationship with the facts.

In John chapter 8, there is the story of the woman caught in the act of adultery. She is brought before Jesus, and, placing her in their midst, the scribes and Pharisees said, "Now, in the Law, Moses commanded us to stone such people. What do you say?" (8:5). Try to imagine putting yourself in the position of this woman. There is no question about whether you are innocent. You're guilty, and now everyone knows it. Perhaps you stopped caring about your innocence long ago. Now, you've been caught offending the law. You were doing something you know is wrong. Everyone is looking at you like you were scum. How humbling! Even if you don't feel ashamed, you might still wish you could hide. You may feel naked. In this woman's case, perhaps, she was somewhat naked. After all, she had been caught in the act of adultery.

Now, put yourself in the position of the Pharisees. You care about nothing but the law and your status in Israel. Jesus has upset your authority. You want to catch Him in some flaw of character, or, in some disagreement with the law. And you're using this pathetic woman to prove you're right. You've brought her to test Jesus.

Perhaps the most upsetting thing about this story is that they act as though she was being adulterous all by herself. All they did was bring the woman! The law says in chapter 22 of Deuteronomy: "You shall bring them both to the gate of that city, and you shall stone them to death with stones" (v. 24). So there must be some man getting off scot-free because all the Pharisees wanted to do was use the woman to catch Jesus. They were using her as nothing more than an object, a thing, an *it*, a nobody. They saw Jesus the same way. He was an object they wanted to get rid of.

And what does Jesus do? He just quietly stoops down and draws in the dirt. Maybe He is writing words, and after each word, he would look up at a particular individual. He would say nothing, just look. Tradition says He was writing down the sins of several of the men there. He'd write "Proud" and then look up at a man who was proud. He'd write "Arrogant," and then look up at another. He'd write "Merciless," "Unbending," "Hypocrite," … and each time, he'd look up at another person. And they'd feel like Jesus had just undressed them. Revealed their hidden secrets. And then He stood up to say, "Let him who is without sin cast the first stone" (v. 7) And everyone there dropped their stones. The humiliation the woman was caused was turned around and thrown right back in their faces.

And then Jesus turned and spoke to the woman. "Where are the people who accused you?" (John 8:10). And they'd all gone away. No one was there to condemn her anymore. And Jesus wouldn't condemn her either. He just said, "Go, and sin no more" (John 8:11).

Whereas before, she was as good as dead, Jesus had given her life. (Here's another example of feeling a resurrection experience!) In every aspect of the word, He saved her. What a change that must have been for that woman. What a feeling it must have been to have been treated like a person and not a thing. Jesus treated her, not as an *it*, but as a *thou* (Martin Buber).

This story from John 8 is a prelude to what I really want to share today. When I was fourteen, I was in the confirmation class at the Winnetka Congregational Church. Don Hagerty was the minister who was leading the class. He was young, about thirty, and he had kept me interested in most of what he had to share. I suppose my primary interest was the cute blonde who always flirted with me. But one day, I felt a conviction, an enlightenment, a great inspiration by what Rev. Hagerty was saying. He talked about the ideas of a man named Martin Buber. He was a Jewish theologian who died in 1965. But Buber had an idea that everything we feel, everything we think, and every act we do is determined by the relationships we have, and the ways we relate. According to Buber, we relate to the world and to persons in two ways. Sometimes we relate to people and things as though they were an *It*. And sometimes, we relate to people and things as though they were a *Thou*. The relationships we have then become I-It relationships, and I-Thou relationships, because it is always an I that is relating.

In an I-It relationship, there is a more of a separation created than a true relationship. Presuming it is I doing the relating, as I act on an It, I keep my distance, using the It for whatever I determine. I can control the object and the object serves my purposes, but I give nothing in return. I am uninvolved. There is no deep feeling on my part for the object. This type of relationship is like scientific study. It is objective. It is manipulative. It is also the attitude of discovery. And it is more of an attitude than it is a relationship. The scribes and Pharisees were treating the woman caught in the act of adultery as an It. Thomas was thinking of the resurrected Jesus more as an It, an object, than as a person.

The I-It relationship is relevant for science, psychology, medical doctors, legal counsel, police, etc. As a system, it is more impersonal, as it needs to be objective. There will always be times when we need that sort of objectivity. But each system, as a system, is not an end in itself. The Pharisees and scribes were using the law as an end in itself, against the woman, and, against Christ. But a system is always meant to lead beyond itself. The moral demands of the law are there to raise us to the sphere of goodness, harmony, and holiness. The intentions of medicine are health, wholeness, and life. The intentions of psychology are happiness, understanding, and awareness. Every system is like a path, but that path also leads to a bridge. And when we get stuck in our own little system, the I-It relationship just doesn't let us cross over that bridge. It holds us back. That doesn't mean that the system is necessarily bad or evil. It can be helpful to have an objective perspective. But that perspective is limited. And so am I when I live only by the I-It attitude. The scribes and Pharisees were limited. The world of I-It is the world where things are merely experienced. The things don't really participate in the experience. And, in fact, we become an It ourselves as we focus on the I-It relationship.

But in the world of I-Thou, there is a purer relation. There is equal give and take. A Thou acts on an I as an I acts on a Thou. To create such a pure relationship, a person must put his or her whole being into the act of relating. It is like putting your soul between you and the person (or thing) with which you are relating, while they put themselves between you and them in mutuality. Now, when it comes to *things*, they can't really relate. So, it is a mistake to treat a thing as a Thou, simply because a thing cannot become a Thou. There can be no mutuality. But in true mutuality is true relationship. There is a connection, a concentration, an intentionality. There is a commitment. The I-Thou relationship is more than an experience; it is an encounter. It is not just a search for particular qualities, but a penetration into being. I see it as a search for the presence of the soul of another.

As Rev. Hagerty explained this way of relating, I began to want to pursue it. As I began to understand the I-Thou relationship, I felt as though I could connect it with the words of scripture, the ultimate vision of the law—to love God with all my heart and mind and strength and soul. And to love my neighbor as myself. To do unto others as I would have others do unto me. It all seemed to be one great universal principle: Treat others as an It and I am an It. Treat others as a Thou, and I too, will become a Thou.

And in every Thou with which I can relate, I can find the presence of the Eternal Thou. The presence of God. As I learned this, I began to believe that if we could all simply treat others as though they were a Thou and not an It, as though God, too, was there in the sharing of our souls, we could all cross over that bridge, go beyond ourselves, beyond this impersonal world to the world of true relationships.

I felt convicted. I wanted to be able to offer this sort of insight to others simply by sharing such truths. I felt called. From that day on, I wanted to be a minister, a pastor, someone whose work was to share the deeper meaning of life, someone who could share the Thou of God and the Thou of myself. It is through sincere relationships that we are moved beyond ourselves. It is through truly relating and caring for people, not treating them as an It, that the depths of life are magnified. And faith is a relationship.

Christianity is not so much a religion as relationships. It is a relationship of people-with-people-with-God! The way of pure relationship is the way of love. Before Christ, no one is an It. And Christ Himself cannot be an It. Thomas discovered the Thou of Christ as He appeared to him and invited him to truly experience Himself, to encounter His Thou. And Thomas was awakened. Thomas was convicted. And we too are convicted, convicted of our blessing. "Blessed are they who have not seen and yet believe!"

I was changed. I don't call it a born-again experience but a conviction experience. I am constantly being born again and again in every experience of another Thou in my life, for therein I find the Eternal Thou as well. God is with us, and, within us. Blessed are they who can see this truth. Blessed are we when we share our souls with one another. Blessed are we when we share the power of the presence of Christ that Thomas met in his encounter. We are blessed. We can encounter Christ in and through each other!

Cast the Net

_____

After these things
Jesus showed himself again to his disciples by the Sea of Tiberius;
and he showed himself in this way.
Gathered there together were Simon Peter, Thomas called the Twin,
Nathanael of Cana in Galilee, the sons of Zebedee, and two others of his disciples.
Simon Peter said to them, "I am going fishing."
They said to him, "We will go with you."
They went out and got into the boat, but that night they caught nothing.
Just after daybreak, Jesus stood on the beach;
but the disciples did not know that it was Jesus.
Jesus said to them, "Children, you have no fish, have you?"
They answered him, "No." He said to them,
"Cast the net to the right side of the boat, and you will find some."
So they cast it, and now they were not able to haul it in
because there were so many fish.
That disciple whom Jesus loved said to Peter,
"It is the Lord!"
When Simon Peter heard that it was the Lord,
he put on some clothes,
for he was naked, and jumped into the sea.
But the other disciples came in the boat, dragging the net full of fish,
for they were not far from the land, only about a hundred yards off.
When they had gone ashore,
they saw a charcoal fire there, with fish on it, and bread.
Jesus said to them, "Bring some of the fish you have just caught."
So Simon Peter went aboard and hauled the net ashore,
full of large fish, a hundred fifty-three of them;
and though there were so many, the net was not torn.
Jesus said to them, "Come and have breakfast."
Now none of the disciples dared to ask him, "Who are you?"
because they knew it was the Lord.
Jesus came and took the bread and gave it to them,
and did the same with the fish.
This was now the third time that Jesus appeared to the disciples
after he was raised from the dead.

—JOHN 21:1–14

"Cast the net on the right side of the boat!" (John 21:6). The resurrected Christ appears to us in the midst of our work and creates fruit from our labors. The whole night had seemed like a waste of time. They had caught nothing. But when Jesus came on the scene, they caught so many fish that they, all seven of them, could barely haul it aboard.

What a difference Christ made to Peter, who, later, pumped so full of excitement, singlehandedly hauled what might have been at least three hundred pounds of fish, plus the water-soaked net, ashore from the boat that had been docked by the coast!

Sometimes, when I think about the stories I have heard about one Christian who seeks to make a real difference in the lives of others, I feel a bit of awe as I imagine ten like that in the same congregation! Or twenty! Or one hundred! Or 153! By the power of the resurrected Christ in our hearts, we can truly haul to Christ the abundant fruits of our labors!

To be in mission is to cast the net. It is to do some labor we know we are capable of doing, and do it in the name of Christ for the sake of others. And when that happens, an abundance results. It may not always be clear as to what exactly compels individuals to want to work to make some difference in the world through their missionary efforts, but each one of us, as followers of Christ, is given the gifts, the tools, to do so.

From among the mission ministries our congregations support, I would like to encourage each member to make a pet project out of at least one of them. Sometimes, there are so many ministries and causes that tug at my heart that I wish I had more time, more money, more ability to apply the tools that I possess to help them out, to work with them, to offer my support.

Nothing offers a better witness to the faith than seeing missions come alive, seeing houses built, wells dug, blankets distributed, the afflicted ministered to, refugees aided, the abused comforted, the sick nurtured, the lost loved, the poor supported, and so on. The amount of charity and service that is done in the world by Christians is mind-boggling, and still there is more to do. You can do it with your pennies, with your rakes and hoes, with your time, with your ears, sometimes even with just your presence. There is so much to do, so many fish to haul ashore, so many differences to make that it seems to me, to do nothing is to sin.

See yourself as a missionary. See yourself wanting to bring some blessing into the lives of others, and you will be compelled to act. You will be inspired to serve. You will want to make some difference in this world. Supporting the work of your local church is a great beginning, but no Christian church exists only for itself. We are here to do for the world what Christ has done for us.

Be creative. Imagine ways to be in mission. It doesn't all have to be hands-on. The easiest way to be in mission is to support other missionaries, other ministries. Wouldn't it be great to say that this is the church that builds houses, or this is the church that sends sawmills, or this is the church that feeds the hungry, heals the sick, clothes the naked, or helps victims of abuse.

Our actions will make others stand up and notice. And they will give glory to our Father who is in heaven as we let our light shine. The difference we make can set an example. The difference we make for others can make a difference in the lives of those who notice our efforts.

Make a difference. Cast the net! Who knows what the fruits of our labor may be. But Christ will make us fruitful!

MEDITATION 48

The Net Was Not Torn

Jesus said to them,
"Bring some of the fish that you have caught."
So Simon Peter went aboard
and hauled the net ashore,
full of large fish, a hundred fifty-three of them;
and though there were so many,
the net was not torn.

—JOHN 21:10–11

I don't do it often, but I'd like to give an allegorical interpretation of these verses. What that means is that I want to look at the story of the great catch, the breakfast on the beach, and the dialogue with Peter from the point of view that they express, symbolically, ideas or principles that are hidden behind the words. It is not unlike the interpretation of a parable. In the parable of the sower, for example, Jesus refers to the field as the world and the seed as the word of faith.

In this story, perhaps the most important character is Peter. Peter represents the church. At least, he is the rock upon which Jesus would build His church. So, to trace the actions of Peter in this story, we can get some idea of a message for the church. The sea is the world, and the disciples had fished all night on the sea and caught no fish. Their fishing is their service, their mission. The net symbolizes obedience, for the disciples obey the instruction of Christ when He simply says, "Cast your net on the right side of the boat, and you will find some" (John 21:6). The great haul of fish that comes as a result is the reward of discipleship. And the breakfast is a symbol of the communion we share. Notice that the boat which carries the faithful disciples is in the world but not of the world, just as Christians are called to be in but not of the world. The boat could simply represent the faith that keeps us above the depths, keeps us from sinking in worldliness.

That the net was not torn is an interesting side note in the story. It could simply symbolize the miraculous aspect of the glorious catch. It could symbolize the remarkable holding power of the disciples. And it could merely represent the mysterious quality of the experience. But if the net symbolizes obedience, and it is obedience that holds the fish the disciples catch through their ministry, perhaps it is obedience that creates the holding power, as well as the hauling power needed by the church and those who are part of her. The beach could represent the presence of the kingdom, or the true place of belonging, for Christ is there with a meal prepared for His disciples.

The allegory is this: The church is in the world, not sinking into the depths of its worldliness but holding above it like a boat on the water. The mission of the church is to fish for people. Not far from where the church is there is the kingdom and the presence of Christ. Christ calls the church from the kingdom and asks if we, the church, have been effective in our efforts. And we answer no. We are not aware that it is Jesus who is asking this until He commands us to try again on the right side of the boat. The obedience of the church creates results. Perhaps it has to do with timing. Day was breaking, just as Christ rose in power with the sun on Easter day. I would say that for the church today, every Sunday is a little Easter. Every Sunday is a new day in the life of the church. Christians adopted Sunday as their day of worship. Before, the sabbath had been from sunset Friday until sunset Saturday, Sunday was described in the New Testament times as "the Lord's Day." So, it is Sunday when the work of faith, especially in worship, is supposed to take place. Either way, I believe the timing of our witness can be of considerable importance. What does the world expect the Christian to be doing on Sunday?

Back to the allegory. The reward for obedience was a great haul. And because of that reward, they knew it was the Lord. That reward got Peter, the church, so excited that he sprang into the sea. The scripture passage does not say that Peter quickly swam ashore to be with Jesus, but that's what it looks like to me. The disciples haul the net on board and row to shore patiently while the church surges ahead toward Christ. Peter, the church, obeys again when Jesus asks the disciples to bring some of the fish they had caught, and he goes over to the boat and singlehandedly brings the whole net and all the fish, large fish, to Christ. It is the church that brings people to Christ. And Christ has a meal already prepared. "Come," he says, "and have breakfast." The invitation is that simple: Come. And throughout the sharing of this simple meal, everyone can't help but know, without having to ask, that they were with the Lord.

After sharing the meal, Peter is invited to walk with Christ upon the beach. Now, remember that Peter is the church, so it is to the church that Jesus asks three times, "Do you love me." And each time, the church responds yes! But notice that it is not enough that the church merely loves its savior. The savior gives the church a mission: Feed my lambs, tend my sheep, feed my sheep. These three may sound like the same thing, but there is a difference between lambs and sheep, and tending and feeding. Lambs are young. The church is to feed the young. But you don't feed the young lambs the same thing you feed the grown sheep. And tending the flock is to keep them cared for, keep them from going astray. This is the mission of the church. Not only are we to fish for people, but we are to care for the flock. And we do this, not because of the flock, but because of our love for Christ. It seems that, in some ways, the motive for caring for the flock has been mixed or confused. The consistency of the church in its care for the flock has been intermittent, if not neglected.

Notice that the love is not a requisite for sharing in the fellowship meal but follows it. And in that special meal is a witness to the resurrected presence of the Lord. In that fellowship the provisions of the church are sustained. The revealing of Christ is a great sustaining provision offered to and by the church. And through the witness of this meal, through the experience of this fellowship, the blessing of love begins, and the miracle of Christ's presence is made undoubtable.

Now the church experiences both a freedom and a captivity. When a church is young, it seems it takes care of itself. It knows a special freedom. And perhaps the early church experienced such a freedom, even though it was oppressed from the outset. It grew gloriously in the first decades. As the church has matured, it seems captive to forces that make it do what it did not want to do and go where it did not want to go. It may not be a worldly force but a force that indicates by what death the church is to glorify God. You see the church, like Peter, is not meant to seek its own glory but the glory of God, of Christ. The ultimate purpose of the church is simply to follow. And to follow sacrificially.

A Walk on the Beach

When they had finished breakfast,
Jesus said to Simon Peter,
"Simon son of John, do you love me more than these?"
He said to him, "Yes, Lord; you know that I love you."
Jesus said to him, "Feed my lambs."
A second time he said to him, "Simon son of John, do you love me?"
He said to him, "Yes, Lord; you know that I love you."
Jesus said to him, "Tend my sheep."
Jesus said to him the third time, "Simon Son of John, do you love me?"
Peter felt hurt because he said to him the third time, "Do you love me?"
And he said to him, "Lord, you know everything;
you know that I love you."
Jesus said to him, "Feed my sheep."
Very truly, I tell you,
when you were younger,
you used to fasten your own belt and go wherever you wished.
But when you grow old, you will stretch out your hands,
and someone else will fasten a belt around you
and take you where you do not wish to go."
(He said this to indicate the kind of death by which he would glorify God.)
After this he said to him,
"Follow me."

—JOHN 21:15–19

"Simon, son of John, do you. love me more than these?" (v. 15). The question. with the emphasis on the object of the verb, here, makes the issue one of loyalty. When Jesus was arrested, at first, Peter fought to defend Jesus. But only hours later, Peter was denying even knowing Jesus. The lack of loyalty amid the threatening reality of Jesus's impending doom was a defensive posture. Peter had relinquished his public devotion to Christ for the sake of his own safety, his own well-being. He didn't want to be rejected for his affiliation to the one who was on trial.

How often this is true for us in the world who would rather not appear to be "religious" when being "religious" would not seem "cool." Particularly in our adolescence and young adult years, when the social pressure to "fit in" seems to override the idea of not belonging to the crowd, people tend to do all they can to avoid standing outside the group. When rejecting the crowd would bring rejection, we choose, rather, to belong to the crowd.

It happened to me when I was fifteen. I was out for football. We'd been having double practices before school began. But it was Saturday. We weren't going to have practice at all the next day. and I commented on the way in from the field that I was looking forward to Sunday and being able to go to church and worship. A guy named Brandon very sarcastically said, "You don't have to go to church to worship God." I felt the joy of my stance being rejected, and all I said was, "Well, I do!" Several other guys laughed. I felt put down. And I didn't like it. From then on, for a long time. I kept my faith to myself and justified doing so by telling myself that it was too personal a thing to mention in a crowd.

Since then, I have learned that, though faith is a very personal thing, there is an all-pervasive reality that we Christians call the kingdom of God. To be in that kingdom is to be set apart from the way of the world. It is to rise above the earthly attitudes of our life in the flesh. Our faith is a belonging to something more special than any other earth-bound group. The belonging we gain is one that gives peace. joy, love, and eternity. And Jesus said, "Blessed are you when others revile you and persecute you and utter all kinds of evil against you falsely on my account. Rejoice and be glad, for your reward is great in heaven, for so they persecuted the prophets who were before you" (Matthew 5:11–12). The witness of our belonging to Christ is a prophetic one.

"Simon, son of John, do you love me?" (v. 16). Now the emphasis is on the verb, the active product of our loyalty. To love Christ is not only to put Him first in our loyalties, but to put Him first in our hearts. But it is also to care with such a magnitude as to be willing to go to any extent to nurture and sustain the relationship. Love ignores the crowd. Love sees nothing other than the relationship. Jesus does not repeat the phrase as it was first stated. He does not include the words "more than these." It is just "Do you love me?"

A love for Jesus should make us want to know Him so well that nothing else matters. Nothing but Jesus becomes the source of our inspiration. Nothing but Jesus becomes the subject of our thoughts. Nothing but Jesus becomes the driving force of our actions. But all too many people only know *about* Jesus. They fall short of truly knowing Him.

Jesus said:

> As the Father has loved me, so have I loved you; abide in my love. If you keep my commandments, you will abide in my love, just as I have kept my Father's commandments and abide in his love. These things I have spoken to you that my joy may be in you, and that your joy may be full. This is my commandment, that you love one another as I have loved you. Greater love has no man than this, that a man lay down his life for his friends. You are my friends if you do what I command you. No longer do I call you servants, for the servant does not know what his master is doing: but I have called you friends, for all that I have heard from my Father I have made known to you. You did not choose me, but I chose you and appointed you that you should go and bear fruit and that your fruit should abide, so whatever you ask the Father in my name, he may give it to you. This I command you, to love one another. (John 15:9–17)

To love is to abide. to go to any extent to nurture and sustain the relationship. Jesus wants us to love Him by loving one another.

When Peter affirmed his love for Jesus the first time, Jesus then told him, "Feed my lambs." Loyalty to Christ is to mean loyalty to His flock. This second time, Christ tells him, "Tend my sheep." The love, nurture, and sustaining care Peter has for Christ is also to be given to the flock.

"Simon, son of John, do you love me?" (v. 17) The emphasis is now on the subject in the question. This time, Peter was grieved. It cut to the root of the matter. Peter is faced with the stabbing thrust of the pain of this sudden, penetrating moment of self-examination. He must ask himself, "Who am I who loves Jesus?" Do I love Him as an admirer? Do I love

Him as I would love a beautiful work of art? Do I love Him with my head and not my heart? With my emotions and not my soul? Do I love Him because of what I get from Him? What is my motive for saying, "I love Jesus?" We need to realize that love is its own motive. True love doesn't love conditionally. It doesn't love simply because I get something out of the relationship. It loves because it gets to give love. It loves because it is so deep within us to feel and do it that to not love is to act contrary to who we are. So, we need to ask ourselves, is my saying, "Yes, Lord," just a matter of giving lip service, or do I really feel devotion and adoration for Him? Is my love a wishful thing or a longing desire? Is my love just brotherly love, or am I passionate about the relationship? Will my love for Jesus be that of just a companion, or will it be that of a soul mate?

We too must examine our love for Christ. We may love Him because we love His kingdom, but do we love Him enough to bear His cross? We may love Him because His grace is so consoling, but do we love Him enough to suffer with Him? We may love Him as we seek His mercy, but do we love Him enough to deny ourselves for the sake of others? We may love Him as we follow His heavenly ways, but do we love Him enough to be sent forth in His name?

Do we love Jesus in such a way that we are more willing to feed His flock than for ourselves to be fed? And when we are fed, does it give us strength enough to seek that nourishment for those who are starving for a good word? What will we do when we've been fed? Apart from giving thanks, that's usually where it ends. We are filled, and yet so much of the world goes hungry.

The time may come when we, like Peter, will be taken where we don't really wish to go. Do we love Christ enough to go all the way for Him?

Feed my sheep. Tend my sheep. Feed my sheep!

MEDITATION 50

Could It Be

A dramatic reading based on John
20:19–25 and Luke 24:13–35.

Characters
John, James, Matthew, Peter, Thomas, Bartholomew, Cleopas, Voice

(The disciples surround Thomas) (Rapidly)
JOHN. But Thomas, He was right here! He is risen!

JAMES. The doors were locked. But somehow, all of a sudden, He was
here!

MATTHEW. (*Serenely*) He said, "Peace be with you!"

PETER. And He showed us His wounds.

JAMES. None of us believed it at first. It was too good to be true! He gave
us His blessing!

MATTHEW. (*Serenely*) He gave us the Holy Spirit!

PETER. He said, "If you forgive the sins of any, they are forgiven!"

JOHN. He gave us His authority!

JAMES. And then He was gone!

JOHN. We have seen the Lord!

THOMAS. (*Angry and resentful; shaking his head through it all*) Unless I
see the mark of the nails in His hands … Unless I touch the wound
in His side … I will not believe! (*Loud knock at the door. Thomas
moves off to the edge of the gathering.*)

PETER. Who could that be?

MATTHEW. They want to arrest us!

JAMES. What should we do?

JOHN. (*Slower now*) Easy now. Let's see who it is. It could be Andrew or Philip or Nathanael.

PETER. (*Goes to the door. Quietly says*) Who is it?

BARTHOLOMEW. (*From outside*) It's Bartholomew and Cleopas.

PETER. (*Opens the door, quickly lets them in, then checks outside to be sure things are secure*) Come in, quickly. Did any of the elders see you come here?

BARTHOLOMEW. (*Quietly at first*) No. We stopped at Cleopas's uncle's home first. Went out the back way … (*Louder and joyfully*) But rejoice! Christ is risen!

JOHN. He is risen indeed!

JAMES AND MATTHEW. Indeed!

MATTHEW. He appeared to Peter!

BARTHOLOMEW. He appeared to me and Cleopas! He walked with us. We were on the road to Emmaus, and He joined us! He traveled with us! But somehow our eyes were kept from recognizing Him.

CLEOPAS. We were talking about Jesus and all the things that happened over the past few days.

BARTHOLOMEW. I told Cleopas about our last supper with the Master …

CLEOPAS. … About His arrest …

PETER. Did you tell him about Judas, who betrayed Jesus?

MATTHEW. Did you tell him how Peter denied even knowing Him?

PETER. (*Hangs his head, shaking it shamefully*)

CLEOPAS. He told me everything. I know you all ran when the arrest happened.

PETER. Jesus wouldn't let us fight for Him!

BARTHOLOMEW. When Jesus joined us on the road, He asked us what we were discussing.

CLEOPAS. At first, all we could do is just stand there. It was hard to hold back the tears. Finally, I spoke up. I said, "Are You the only stranger in Jerusalem who doesn't know what's happened there?"

BARTHOLOMEW. And He said, "What things?" He wanted to hear how we remembered it all.

CLEOPAS. We told Him, "The things about Jesus of Nazareth, who was a mighty prophet in both word and deed, spoken well of before God and all the people."

BARTHOLOMEW. And we told Him how the chief priests and the elders handed Him over to be crucified by the Romans.

JOHN. It wasn't even a real trial.

MATTHEW. They stirred up some of the people in the crowd to call for His crucifixion!

PETER. They asked for Barabbas to be released and for Jesus to be condemned!

CLEOPAS. We told Him that it was now the third day since our Lord had died.

BARTHOLMEW. And that some of the women among us had astounded us.

JAMES. Yes. They had gone to His tomb at first light. When they didn't find His body there, they saw angels, they said, "He is not here!" They told them Jesus was alive!

JOHN. He is risen!

JAMES. He is risen indeed!

BARTHOLOMEW. Angels?

CLEOPAS. A vision?

PETER. More than a vision! Some of us went to the tomb and found it just as they said. It was empty. He wasn't there!

BARTHOLOMEW. We told all this to the stranger.

CLEOPAS. But He told us how foolish we are.

BARTHOLOMEW. "Was it not necessary," He said, "that the Messiah should suffer these things before He enters into His glory?"

CLEOPAS. Then beginning with Moses ... and then prophet by prophet, He interpreted what had happened to Himself as the fulfillment of the scriptures.

BARTHOLOMEW. When we got close to Emmaus, it seemed like He would have kept on. But we invited Him to come with us.

CLEOPAS. We wanted to hear more. Couldn't get enough of it.

BARTHOLOMEW. My heart was burning within me.

CLEOPAS. Mine too. Every word He said, every passage He shared. It was like it was being written on my heart!

MATTHEW. What passages?

BARTHOLOMEW. From Isaiah, especially, the vision of the Suffering Servant!

VOICE. (Reads Isaiah 53:3–10).

PETER. The resurrection! Didn't He tell us that He would rise?

JOHN. More than once! And He said it would be in fulfillment of the scriptures!

BARTHOLOMEW. Well, He didn't want to impose.

CLEOPAS. But we urged Him strongly, because it was almost sunset, the day was nearly over.

BARTHOLOMEW. So, He joined us. It was Cleopas's house.

CLEOPAS. I prepared some bread and fruit, with a little wine.

BARTHOLOIVEW. He sat with us at the table. He took the bread and, holding it up,

said a blessing! And when He broke it, and gave it to us.

CLEOPAS. Our eyes were opened!

BARTHOLOMEW. The wounds in His hands!

CLEOPAS. We recognized Him!

BARTHOLOMEW. Before we could catch our breath, though … He was gone!

CLEOPAS. In an instant!

BARTHOLOMEW. Vanished out of sight!

CLEOPAS. Bartholomew looked at me, and I looked at Him …

BARTHOLOMEW AND CLOEPAS. (*together*) *He is risen!*

BARTHOLOMEW. We said it together!

CLEOPAS. And then we laughed out loud and said …

CLEOPAS AND BARTHOLOMEW. (*together*) We've got to tell the others!

BARTHOLOVIEW. So. Here we are! (*Pause. All freeze except Thomas.*)

THOMAS. (*Steps forward*) Could it be …? Christ is risen?

ALL. Indeed!

CONCLUSION

The resurrection of Christ has changed everything. It changes our outlook on death. It changes our perspective on healing. It changes the whole way we look at this world. And it changes us—our hearts, our minds, our hopes, our fears. It's as if we are in fact awakened from a sleep so deep that it kept us from knowing who was in the room with us keeping watch over us while we recovered from our wounds.

And even though we may never have known we were wounded, the change is real as if we were brought from darkness into the light, from pain to comfort, from brokenness to wholeness, from a prison cell to complete freedom, from poverty to wealth, from sin to forgiveness. It is a whole new life. Paul describes our changed condition by saying, "For once you were darkness, but now you are light." And he sets a standard for us by saying, "Walk as children of the light, for the fruit of light is found in all that is good and right and true; and try to learn what is pleasing to the Lord" (Ephesians 5:8–10).

In Romans 12:2, Paul tells us: "Do not be conformed to this world, but be transformed by the renewal of your mind, that you may prove what is the will of God, what is good and acceptable and perfect." David Caldwell of the West-Ark Church of Christ in Fort Smith, Arkansas, speaks of what he calls the resurrection principle. He says, "The fact of the resurrection verifies the resurrection principle. The resurrection principle prepares the believer to live with God. Christians allow God to resurrect their minds and hearts now so that He can resurrect their bodies later. The resurrection principle is activated when sin is destroyed by forgiveness."

May the fact of the resurrection of Christ inspire you to live by the resurrection principle! May the power of God revealed in the glory of Easter have its effects on you! And may the grace that raised our Lord and savior Jesus Christ from the dead fill your hearts and minds till you are made completely new.

"Lo, I tell you a mystery ... We shall not all sleep, but we shall all be changed, in a moment, in the twinkling of an eye, at the last trumpet. For the trumpet will sound, and the dead will be raised imperishable, and we shall all be changed!" (1 Corinthians 15:51–52).

Once, we were darkness, but now we are light!

Let it shine!

The Power of His Resurrection

Yet whatever gains I had,
these I have come to regard as loss because of Christ.
More than that, I regard everything as loss
because of the surpassing value of knowing Christ Jesus my Lord.
For his sake I have suffered the loss of all things,
and I regard them as rubbish,
in order that I may gain Christ and be found in him,
not having a righteousness of my own that comes from the law,
but one that comes through faith in Christ,
the righteousness from God based on faith.
I want to know Christ and the power of his resurrection
and the sharing of his sufferings
by becoming like him in his death,
if somehow I may attain the resurrection from the dead,
Not that I have already obtained this
or have already reached the goal;
but I press on to make it my own,
because Christ Jesus has made me his own.
Beloved, I do not consider that I have made it my own;
but this one thing I do:
forgetting what lies behind and straining forward to what lies ahead,
I press on toward the goal
for the prize of the heavenly call of God in Christ Jesus.
Let those of us then who are mature be of the same mind;
and if you think differently about anything,
this too God will reveal to you.
Only let us hold fast to what we have attained.
Yet whatever gain I had,
these I have come to regard as loss because of Christ.
More than that, I regard everything as loss
because of the surpassing value of knowing Christ Jesus my Lord.
For his sake I have suffered the loss of all things,

and I regard them as rubbish,
in order that I may gain Christ and be found in him,
not having a righteousness of my own that comes from the law,
but one that comes through faith in Christ,
the righteousness from God based on faith.
I want to know Christ and the power of his resurrection
and the sharing of his sufferings
by becoming like him in his death,
if somehow I may attain the resurrection from the dead.
Not that I have already obtained this or have already reached the goal;
but I press on to make it my own,
because Christ Jesus has made me his own.
Beloved, I do not consider that I have made it my own;
but this one thing I do:
forgetting what lies behind and straining forward to what lies ahead,
I press on toward the goal
for the prize of the heavenly call of God in Christ Jesus.
Let those of us then who are mature be of the same mind;
and if you think differently about anything,
this too God will reveal to you.
Only let us hold fast to what we have attained.

—PHILIPPIANS 3:7–16

Imagine you're on the outside looking in. Imagine that what you see is people who are happy, people who are loving, people who are kind and comforting, people who are helpful, people who are self-giving, people who know Jesus Christ. They are people who follow His way and do His will. They are people who know Him as Lord, not just as a savior. They are people who honor Christ and glorify Him in all they say and do. But they're in *there*, and you are not. How do you feel? Do you feel as though you belong in there? What would you do to get in there? Would you give up whatever it is that keeps you outside?

What if somehow you lost all the material things you had, or, thought you had. What would you have left? You might still have your emotions, your thoughts, your dreams, your memories. You might still have your friends, relatives, and associates. But what if some of those relationships are holding you back, keeping you from being like the people on the "inside"?

I COUNT EVERYTHING AS LOSS

Paul was able to say: "Whatever gain I had, I counted as loss for the sake of Christ. Indeed I count everything as loss because of the surpassing worth of knowing Christ Jesus my Lord. For His sake I have suffered the loss of all things, and count them as rubbish, in order that I may gain Christ and be found in Him!" (Philippians 3:7–9). Anything we might have becomes worthless in the light of the surpassing worth of knowing Jesus as Lord. All our achievements, all our possessions, all our earthly wealth is literally nothing compared to the grace of Jesus Christ!

NOT HAVING RIGHTEOUSNESS OF MY OWN

Paul wanted a righteousness based on faith in Christ. He wanted it so that he might "know Him and the power of His resurrection" (v. 10). Do you know the power of Christ's resurrection? Do you know what it is that gives new life? Do you know what it is that conquers death, that opens the way to the kingdom of eternal life? How do you experience it? How do you understand this power? Look at what Paul says: "That I may know Him and the power of His resurrection, and may share His sufferings, becoming like Him in His death, that if possible, may attain the resurrection of the dead!" (v. 10–11).

We are virtually on the outside looking in. We are looking in on eternity. We know a bit about what eternity holds, who enters eternity, and how they would behave. We know it now, but we fall short in living it here.

NOT THAT I AM ALREADY PERFECT

You see, we know, as did Paul, that we are not there yet. He said, "Not that I have already obtained this or am already perfect (reached the goal)" (v. 12). It's not over … till it's over. All too often, we live as if we had the ticket, and as if all we had to do was have a ticket. But having a ticket and entering the banquet are not the same thing. We may know the power of Christ's resurrection. We may know how wonderful it is to have experienced the amazing grace of His love and forgiveness. We may even have had an experience of assurance about the gift of eternal life. But we are not there yet. We are not finished yet.

I PRESS ON

"Not that I have already obtained this or am already perfect; but I press on to make it my own" (v. 12). Why? "Because Christ Jesus has made me His own!" (12b). We become satisfied. We become complacent, thinking that we have done enough to get to heaven, when all we have is a ticket to the banquet. People with a ticket are supposed to behave a certain way. The clues to this certain type of behavior comes in what Paul said back in verse 10. It has to do with sharing in Christ's sufferings!

Sufferings! That doesn't sound like heaven! No, but it has everything to do with the path that leads there. The power of Christ's resurrection is connected to the suffering of Christ's cross. I've said elsewhere that there is no resurrection if there is no cross. And Jesus said, "If any one would come after me, let them deny themselves and take up their cross and follow me" (Matthew 16:24). The suffering to be considered, the cross to be borne, is the weight of our mission, the burden of our love, the struggle of our service. At a minimum, the sacrificial suffering we can offer is the relinquishment of our own designs for the designs of Christ. Doing, not for ourselves, but unto others. Once we become believers, Christ begins to work His way into our personality, our attitudes, and our actions. The goal is to live in such a way that when others see us, they see Christ. When others see us, they should be able to know more about Jesus Christ. If not, at least, they will see us pressing on to make Him our own.

THE UPWARD CALL

"Brothers and sisters, I do not consider that I have made it my own; but one thing I do, forgetting what lies behind and straining forward to what lies ahead, I press on toward the goal for the prize of the upward call of God in Christ Jesus." (vv. 13–14). It is nice, sometimes, to watch the figure skaters on television. They move with such grace and beauty. But what we, who sit and watch them perform, do not see is the hours and hours of daily practice that go into making them look so perfect. Even when they've done a routine perfectly in the past, they continue to practice to be able to do it again. There is a prize, an earthly prize, for which they compete. But we, the faithful, strive for that upward call. We strive (press on) for excellence in our faith, for grace and beauty in our lives. And we must do this by practicing our faith. Faith is not a thing to be grasped like a possession, or won like a prize; it is an art to be practiced, a gift to be shared, a talent to be exercised, a strength to be used.

You see, it is not only for ourselves that we experience the power of Christ's resurrection, but for others. Our faith can make a difference in another's life. We do not serve ourselves; we serve Christ, who suffered for others, who gave His life, His love, His care, not for His own reward, but that we might be able to receive His gift of eternal life, resurrected life, new life. This is our upward (heavenly) call.

JUSTIFYING GRACE AND SANCTIFYING GRACE

Two types of grace are at work in a believer's life. First there is what is called justifying grace. This is the grace that saves, that changes us, that makes us right with God. But there is also sanctifying grace. This is the grace that produces fruits. When Christ spoke of how the tree is known by its fruits, he was not speaking of a works righteousness, but of the result of having received grace. A believer's life produces fruits consistent with the life of Christ. We can be very happy to have been justified; it's a glorious thing. But our response of love for Christ should compel us to do for others what we feel Christ has done for us.

HOLD TRUE

"Let those of us who are mature be thus minded; and if in anything you are otherwise minded, God will reveal that also to you. Only let us hold true (or hold fast) to what we have attained" (v. 15–16) There is to be no falling back. Backsliding is a sin. It's like losing the ticket! We must hold true to what we have attained, or our faith was never more than superficial. We still need to be justified by grace. And what we do comes as a natural result of who we are in Christ.

Press on, let the grace of God work in you in such a way that you continually strive to become complete, to become like Christ. For it is by His power—the power of His resurrection—that we are walking now. Our lives belong to Him. We must give ourselves over, and then He will become ours!

It's a wonderful mystery: give yourself to Christ, and Christ will give Himself to you. If you don't believe it, press on, and God will reveal that also to you! Only let us hold true to what we have attained, to the power of His resurrection!

That's all (for now)!

Printed in the United States
by Baker & Taylor Publisher Services